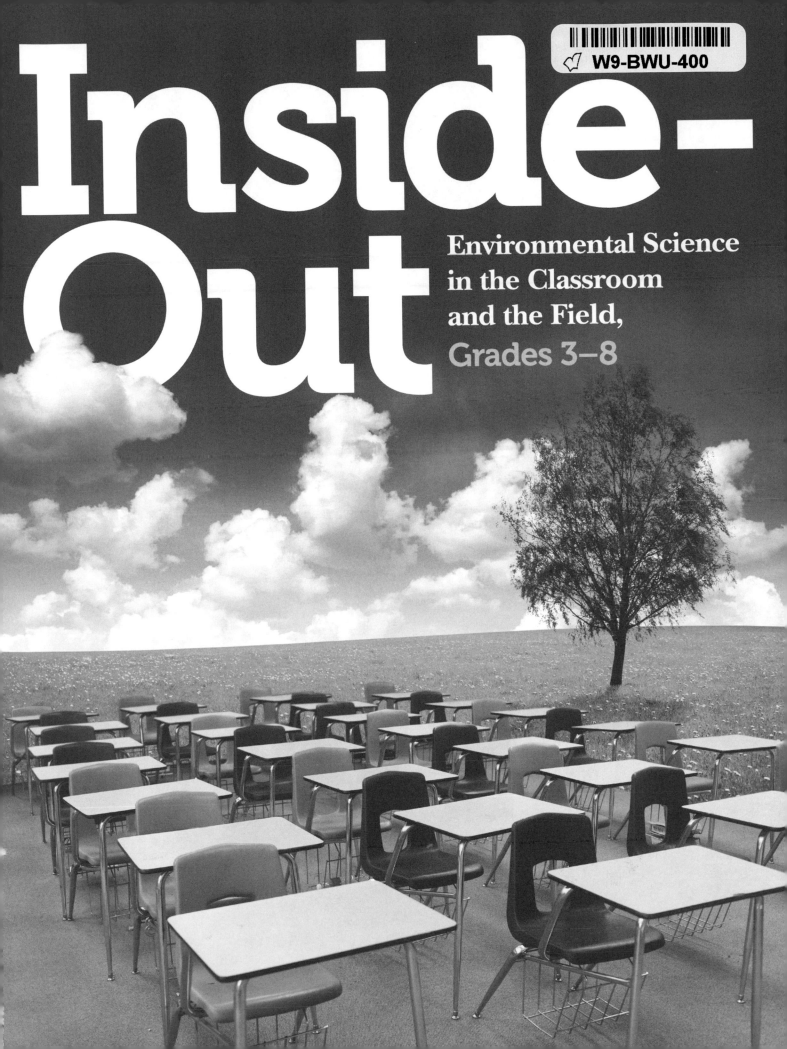

Inside-Out

Environmental Science in the Classroom and the Field,

Grades 3–8

Inside-Out

Environmental Science in the Classroom and the Field, Grades 3–8

Robert W. Blake Jr.
J. Adam Frederick
Sarah Haines
Stephanie Colby Lee

NSTApress

National Science Teachers Association

Arlington, Virginia

National Science Teachers Association

Claire Reinburg, Director
Jennifer Horak, Managing Editor
Andrew Cocke, Senior Editor
Judy Cusick, Senior Editor
Wendy Rubin, Associate Editor
Amy America, Book Acquisitions Coordinator

ART AND DESIGN
Will Thomas Jr., Director
Joe Butera, Senior Graphic Designer, cover and interior design
Cover photos by Iakov Kalinin and Andrew Manley for iStock

PRINTING AND PRODUCTION
Catherine Lorrain, Director

SCILINKS
Tyson Brown, Director
Virginie L. Chokouanga, Customer Service and Database Coordinator

NATIONAL SCIENCE TEACHERS ASSOCIATION
Francis Q. Eberle, PhD, Executive Director
David Beacom, Publisher

Copyright © 2010 by the National Science Teachers Association.
All rights reserved. Printed in the United States of America.
12 11 10 09   4 3 2 1

Library of Congress Cataloging-in-Publication Data
Inside-out : Environmental science in the classroom and the field, grades 3-8 / Robert W. Blake ... [et al.].
    p. cm.
 Includes bibliographical references.
 ISBN 978-1-935155-11-9
 1. Environmental sciences--Study and teaching (Elementary)--Activity programs. 2. Environmental sciences--Study and teaching
(Middle school)--Activity programs. 3. Environmental education. 4. Fieldwork (Educational method) I. Blake, Robert W., 1961-
 GE70.I575 2009
 372.35'7--dc22

                    2009051811

 eISBN 978-1-936137-79-4

PERMISSIONS
You may photocopy, print, or e-mail up to five copies of an NSTA book chapter for personal use only; this does not include display or promotional use. Elementary, middle, and high school teachers *only* may reproduce a single NSTA book chapter for classroom or noncommercial, professional-development use only. For permission to photocopy or use material electronically from this NSTA Press book, please contact the Copyright Clearance Center (CCC) (*www.copyright.com*; 978-750-8400). Please access *www.nsta.org/permissions* for further information about NSTA's rights and permissions policies.

Featuring SciLinks—a new way of connecting text and the Internet. Up-to-the-minute online content, classroom ideas, and other materials are just a click away. For more information, go to www.scilinks.org/Faq.aspx.

Contents

Contents

Contents

Chapter 8
Reflections on Implementation

Dedication

To our parents

Dr. Robert W. and Carol Blake
Dr. A. Bruce and Norma N. Frederick
Bonnie and Gary Rogers
Margaret and Charles P. Colby Jr.

For providing our childhood with opportunities and
the freedom to explore the outdoors

Acknowledgments

The impetus for this project was a 2002 Eisenhower Grant, and the book idea was launched after NSTA's national conference in Philadelphia in 2003. We realized then that our emphasis on increased content knowledge, combined with a passion for outdoor learning, was a key to both teacher and student engagement in high-quality, meaningful learning experiences in environmental science. Our combined 60 years of science teaching experience at all levels of the professional continuum convinced us that what we had to say was significant and timely. However, to dare say that what we present here is all our own is against our fundamental belief that "the reason we can see for miles is because we stand on the shoulders of giants." Without such giants, or those that came before, the task of writing this book would have been close to impossible. Thus, in our attempt to acknowledge those we can readily remember, we will also most likely fail to mention many more who have shaped our thinking and practice along the way.

We first would like to thank those granting agencies that believed in our ideas as we engage teachers and students in field-based learning. These include the U.S. Department of Education with the Maryland Higher Education Commission (Eisenhower Grant program, award number E01-21-113), the National Oceanic and Atmospheric Administration (NOAA, award number NA03NMF4570216)[1], the American Forest Foundation (AFF) and Project Learning Tree (PLT), and the Chesapeake Bay Trust. Without these critical funds we would not have been able to pursue our passion.

---

[1] Award number NA03NMF4570216 from the National Oceanic and Atmospheric Administration, U.S. Department of Commerce. The statements, findings, conclusions, and recommendations are those of the author(s) and do not necessarily reflect the views of the National Oceanic and Atmospheric Administration or the Department of Commerce.

Acknowledgments

As you read this book, you will also find resources from a wide array of agencies and organizations related to science education. As we explain in the introduction, web-based resources are almost endless, thus it is difficult to acknowledge all that have affected our work. Having said this, and although many web-based materials are of public domain, we still would like to thank specific groups that gave us permission to use their materials. These include the Maryland Department of Natural Resources, the Virginia Save Our Streams Program, the United States Geological Service, the University of Rhode Island, the Maryland Sea Grant College program, the Chesapeake Bay Program, the National Oceanic and Atmospheric Administration, Environmental Concern, the Laboratory for Atmospheric and Space Physics, the University of Colorado, and BioWorld Products LLC (Visalia, CA).

Next, we would like to thank those in the peer review process, all of whom contributed significant time and effort to provide well-constructed feedback and suggestions for revisions. Although we did not agree with all comments about changes to the text, this process did shape the final format, and we greatly value the practice and acknowledge that the book is better for it. We also wish to thank the editors for supporting our belief that content knowledge is a prerequisite to meaningful learning. While we realize that "knowing" does not guarantee high-quality teaching, content understanding does provide confidence in creating varied learning experiences for children.

Laboratory experiences that are directly linked to field-based inquiry are essential for the overall learning process in science. We thank Jeff Morgen, the former science education specialist at the SciTech education program of the Center of Marine Biotechnology (COMB), located in Baltimore, Maryland, for providing such experiences. Without Jeff's leadership and "can do" attitude we would not have been able to provide laboratory and field-based learning for elementary teachers, interns, and students.

We also would like to acknowledge additional contributors to this book. We thank Debbie Freels, Mark Herzog, Steve Lev, Pam Lottero-Perdue, and Christine Wolfe for their help.

A big thank-you must go to Carminantonio and Bruna Iannaccone for providing an essential respite and excellent food that can only be found at the Piedigrotta Bakery in Baltimore, Maryland.

We are greatly indebted to Patricia Freedman for her editorial skills. Her dogged tenacity and exceptional humor, as well as her tolerance of our numerous inane mistakes and simple decency for not bringing attention to our own shortcomings, made this monotonous process tolerable.

Finally, we thank our families for their understanding and contributions to this task. Specifically, we thank Dr. Robert W. Blake, Sr., and Dr. A. Bruce Frederick for their input and editorial skills. We thank our wives, Jennifer Blake and Lisa Frederick, and our husbands, Tom Haines and John Lee, for unwavering support. We thank our children—MacKenzie Blake; Christopher, David, and Elaina Frederick; and Andrew and Adam Haines—for their continued interest in spontaneous field-experiences that persist to remind us of the importance of these learning experiences.

Safety Practices

Safety Out-of-Doors Practices

1. Teachers should always visit out-of-doors areas to review potential safety hazards prior to students' carrying out activities.

2. Keep clear of out-of-doors areas that may have been treated with pesticides, fungicides, and other hazardous chemicals.

3. When working out-of-doors, students should use appropriate personal protective equipment (PPE), including safety glasses or goggles (when working with hazardous chemicals), gloves, close-toed shoes, hat, long-sleeve shirt and pants, sunglasses, and sunscreen protection. When working near deep water, use life preservers or other floatation devices.

4. Caution students relative to poisonous plants (ivy, sumac, etc.), insects (bees, wasps, ticks, mosquitoes, etc.), and hazardous debris (broken glass, other sharps, etc.).

5. Caution students about trip and fall hazards such as rocks, string or rope, and so on when walking out-of-doors.

6. Teachers need to inform parents in writing of on-site field trips relative to potential hazards and safety precautions being taken.

7. Teachers need to check with the school nurse about student medical issues such as allergies, asthma, and so on. Be prepared for medical emergencies.

8. Teachers need to have a form of communication available, such as a cell phone or two-way radio, in case of emergency.

9. Wash hands with soap and water after doing activities dealing with hazardous chemicals, soil, biologicals (insects, leaves, etc.), or other materials, as well as after returning to the classroom from out-of-doors activities.

10. Contact the main office before bringing classes out of the building for activities.

Safety in the Classroom Practices

1. When working with glassware, metersticks, hazardous chemicals (including soil testing kits), and so on, students should use appropriate personal protective equipment (PPE), including indirectly vented chemical splash goggles, gloves, and aprons.

2. Always review Material Safety Data Sheets (MSDS) with students relative to safety precautions in working with hazardous chemicals.

3. When dealing with hazardous chemicals, an eyewash station is required should a splash accident in the eyes occur.

4. When heating liquids, use only heat-resistant glassware (Pyrex- or Kimax-type equipment).

5. When heating liquids on electrical equipment such as hot plates, use ground fault protected circuits, or GFI.

6. Always remind students of heat and burn hazards when working with heat sources such as hot plates and light bulbs.

7. Wash hands with soap and water after doing activities dealing with hazardous chemicals, soil, biologicals (insects, leaves, etc.), or other materials.

Introduction

My grandmother, Mary E. E. Kready, took to the field early in the morning just outside of West Chester Normal School (est. 1871) in the spring of 1924. This was a favorite activity of the 18-year-old undergraduate student, not because she needed samples of plant material for her field botany class but—very simply—because she loved it. The serenity, peacefulness, and sense-provoking environment are what she longed for. Nothing was required but her sense of wonder, her sense of place. Surrounded by the inspiration of towering oaks and peeking bloodroot, Mary was at home. Probably very little interference entered her world once in the wooded realm. On this particular day she was searching for elusive ginger to add to her collection. Although it was nearly invisible to the passerby, Mary found the ginger and added it to her field bag with no doubt a great sense of triumph, then continued on her trek.

As I sift through my grandmother's herbarium paper samples, so cleanly preserved and so neatly pressed,

Bloodroot, a sure sign of spring

it gives me great pause and the realization that we must carry stories like this forward to better our teaching and learning of science in our schools and to develop educators with a thirst to walk as Mary did.

J. Adam Frederick, May 2008

Why This Book and Why This Way?

Why an Emphasis on Content?

Children love the outdoors and have many questions pertaining to their natural surroundings, but all too often in elementary and middle schools either students learn very little science in the classroom or the time is usually spent on textbook and direct classroom instruction (NRC Committee on Science Learning, Kindergarten Through Eighth Grade 2007). As an elementary teacher you are

A 1924 yearbook photograph of Mary E. E. Kready at West Chester Normal School

a generalist, expected to know a lot about many topics and to teach many subjects. Unfortunately, when it comes time to teach students science, many of you probably feel unprepared in both content understanding and your ability to provide students with meaningful experiences in science and to actively engage them within the learning process. The lack of content understanding and the ability to know how to apply this knowledge in learning can be an impediment to you and your ability to integrate content with activities. Our fundamental aim for this book, therefore, is to enhance your understanding of basic environmental science concepts and to instill confidence in your ability to engage students in the process of science and learning experiences both inside and outside your classroom.

Why the Elementary Level?

Our use of the term *teacher* is inclusive of both inservice and preservice educators in the elementary and middle school classrooms. Within the concept of *lifelong learner* the National Science Foundation (NSF) coined the term *Teacher Professional Continuum* (TPC); the purpose of the TPC program is to "improve the quality and coherence of teacher learning experiences across the continuum" (NSF 2006). In the current education environment we hear of a need for better STEM (science, technology, engineering, and mathematics) experiences for students and a need for better teachers of STEM subjects. Much of the emphasis on improving STEM education and educators is at the undergraduate and high school levels and on the preparation of those going into STEM professions. Unfortunately, this discussion does not include much talk about the need for better science teaching at the elementary grades and, most important, the need for enhancing a scientific worldview, a viewpoint that is impor-

Introduction

tant for the intellectual capabilities of all people in all walks of life. If we truly believe in a continuum, then helping you, the elementary teacher, learn science content and then use the content to engage students in meaningful and active learning experiences will provide a critical foundation for an overall STEM initiative.

Why Field-Based Learning?

Research and Field-Based Learning

The National Science Education Standards (NRC 1996, p. 13) encourage teachers to help students "experience the richness and excitement of knowing about and understanding the natural world" and "use appropriate scientific processes and principles in making personal decisions." From a research perspective there are a variety of studies indicating that taking students outside to study and understand the natural world is beneficial to their learning. For example, Hungerford and Volk (1990) demonstrated that exposing students to environmental investigations resulted in positive changes in behavior toward the environment. Research by Lieberman and Hoody (1998) and others (Bartosh 2003; Falco 2004; NEETF 2000; SEER 2000) suggests that using the environment as an integrating context for learning (the EIC Model) leads to a host of positive outcomes for students and teachers, including greater academic achievement in reading, mathematics, science, and social studies; increased motivation to learn; and decreased disciplinary issues.

Duffin, Powers, Tremblay, and PEER Associates (2004) reported that the more students are exposed to the EIC approach, the greater their attachment to a sense-of-place ("a special collection of qualities and characteristics, visual, cultural and environmental that provides meaning to location"; Project Learning Tree 2006, p.

25), involvement in environmental stewardship, actual time spent outside, and degree of civic engagement. Additional studies indicate that constructing and maintaining schoolyard gardens is an excellent means for increasing student science achievement scores ("Youth in Horticulture" 2005). For those students diagnosed with attention deficit/hyperactivity disorder, Taylor and Kuo (2009) suggested that simply providing walks in a natural setting increases attentiveness of this particular group of students.

Finally, Louv (2005), in his book *Last Child in the Woods*, coined the term *nature deficit disorder*. Louv described a trend in today's society in which children are not spending significant amounts of time outdoors being exposed to nature. He claimed that there are complex reasons for this phenomenon, which can lead to a host of academic and health-related problems for our youth. Perhaps partially in response to the attention garnered by *Last Child in the Woods* and the groundswell of public opinion that has resulted from it, the U.S. House of Representatives voted on and passed H.R. 3036, the No Child Left Inside Act of 2008 (September 18, 2008). Of the eight main objectives of the bill, four link directly to the purposes of our book:

- To "create opportunities for enhanced and ongoing professional development" in environmental science

- To ensure that environmental education programs are aligned with national, state, and local content standards, to promote "interdisciplinary courses that include strong field components"

- To "bring teachers into contact with working environmental professionals"

- To "establish programs to prepare teachers to provide environmental education professional development to their colleagues and programs to promote outdoor education activities as part of the regular school curriculum" (H.R. 3036—110th Congress 2007)

An Elementary School Principal and Field-Based Learning

Taking all of these reports and studies into consideration, we believe that Debbie Freels, a former elementary school principal, says it best:

As an elementary school principal, I cannot recall hearing about any student not wanting to go outside for an activity! Students yearned for the opportunity to be outdoors during the

school day. By providing instruction through project-based teaching and learning, teachers were able to integrate cross-curricular objectives in science-oriented projects.

I remember conducting formal observations of a teacher teaching a measurement lesson in the field behind the school and of another teacher who taught a writing lesson on descriptive words as students gazed at the changing leaves on the trees on a fall day. Students and teachers alike were energized by being able to extend instruction beyond the walls of the school. Teachers and parents both found that when students were provided with instruction that addressed

Dr. Robert Blake and preservice teachers exploring a stream on the Towson University campus

cross-curriculum content within a science theme and the outdoors was utilized as a classroom, student interest, enthusiasm, and engagement increased as students saw connections between their classroom and the real world. In addition, most students experienced greater academic achievement and understood the importance of environmental stewardship and giving back to the community. I truly believe that these experiences will help to shape future citizens who not only care about the environment, but actively participate in preserving it. (e-mail to Robert Blake, October 22, 2009)

A Practical Reason for Field-Based Learning

Although we often hear from teachers that there "isn't time," "it's not in my curriculum," or "it's not within my structural obligation," it is quite clear from the perspective of both researchers and administrators" that integrated outdoor learning for teachers and students has many benefits, both academic and emotional. In addition, going outside—while rarely an educational objective—is just plain fun, and having fun is one way to increase motivation. Increased motivation leads to greater student and teacher involvement and creates ownership of activities and projects. As Debbie Freels implies, these experiences can be active, integrated, contextualized, and meaningful, allowing both you and your students to move beyond the classroom walls and investigate ideas outside.

Why So Many Web Resources?

As teachers we value the almost unlimited amount of resources available on the World Wide Web, yet we have also struggled with finding pertinent and useful information within a relatively short period of time. We have spent years searching for material that is useful, trustworthy, and relevant for our own teaching. Recently a colleague received the following e-mail from a 30-year veteran of marine education at Oregon Sea Grant who was openly frustrated at not locating curricular information on the web about climate change:

What was causing my frustration, was that I was searching the web using the search words "climate change curriculum... and climate change teaching activities" and finding not much of anything.... Wrong headed. When entered NOAA education, EPA education, NASA education, NANOOS, and MBARI also has an education section with climate change..... a whole new world has opened up. Lots of stuff. One of the sites directed me to NSTA "NSTA Sci Links" which has reviewed science teaching materials and links to what they consider the best. There was also climate change listed there as well. (Vicki Osis, marine educator [retired], Hatfield Marine Science Center, Oregon State University, September 15, 2009)

This is just one example of how difficult it can be to find relevant web-based material quickly, and it shows that although web material may be "easily accessible," it is not always a simple matter of using what you find.

The web resources presented here are a culmination of literally years of searching the web for useful information in environmental science. We know that these resources do not represent everything that is available, but they do represent the best that we have found so far. Certainly more web resources will become available, and some will disappear. We encourage you to continue to "surf the web" looking for useful information for your teaching. However, if time is of the essence, what we provide here will get you started.

Introduction

Concerns Over Regionalism

Our activities focus on the context of our geographic region, with an emphasis on the Chesapeake Bay and its associated watersheds. Providing students who live in the Chesapeake Bay watershed with a "meaningful watershed experience" is a stated goal of the Chesapeake 2000 agreement (Chesapeake Bay Program 2000) and has become a priority for the Maryland State Department of Education. However, the information and activities that we present can be applied to any local ecosystem in different states and different watersheds around the country. For example, if we lived in western New York or western Pennsylvania our watershed focus could be one of the Great Lakes (Lake Erie or Lake Ontario). If we lived in the Seattle, Washington, area we could study Puget Sound. The goals of environmental education and preservation are similar regardless of locale, and the activities in this book are generic enough to apply across various locations and scales.

Why the Environment and Why the Field?

As science educators our purpose with this book is to engage you, teachers of elementary and middle school students, in field-based activities that integrate the scientific disciplines inherent in the study of the environment (Earth science, chemistry, physical geography, and life science). An essential part of this multidisciplinary approach is to better understand the intertwined relationship between the abiotic and biotic factors within an ecosystem and how this can be communicated more clearly. We want you to move your students out of the classroom and into the field to study the natural and physical world through direct observation and inquiry. We also want to help you become comfortable with conducting laboratory and classroom activities that complement and inform field-based learning. Ultimately, it is what you do with your students that will have the greatest impact on them as lifelong learners.

Organization of the Book

Why This Way?

Over the years our work as science educators in preservice teacher preparation and inservice professional development has allowed us to conduct numerous workshops and fieldwork related to the study of the environment. The material in this book represents our current best synthesis of the science content and classroom-tested activities and presents them in an order that we deem useful for teachers. Most of the experiences presented here are based on our work in Professional Development Schools[1], which includes continuous faculty development and preservice teacher preparation.

We want to emphasize the different nature of our presentation. We focus on the content for the simple reason that we believe that content understanding is essential for good teaching. While simply "knowing" does not ensure high-quality teaching, knowing about what you teach is certainly better than not knowing. We also want to emphasize that this is not a curriculum guide or a unit to be followed in a linear sequence. Although we like the sequence, each chapter can stand alone, with you the teacher deciding on what to read, what to use, and in

---

[1] "A Professional Development School (PDS) is a collaboratively planned and implemented partnership for the academic and clinical preparation of interns and the continuous professional development of both school system and institution of higher education (IHE) faculty. The focus of the PDS partnership is improved student performance through research-based teaching and learning." (Maryland State Department of Education 2007)

what order. We strongly believe in your professionalism and your quest for continuing to better your teaching and the experiences that you provide for your students. We provide but one model and one pathway of how to engage teachers and students in field- and laboratory-based activities that promote inquiry and project-based learning. Ultimately, it is you who will make the decisions of what to use as you seek to engage your students in meaningful learning.

Chapter Organization

In Chapters 1–7, we will first discuss and display the content material of each chapter title and then present activities that engage students in learning and applying the content knowledge. Activities are mainly field based but do include a number of classroom-based laboratory-type settings. Each activity follows a generalized format to promote student inquiry. This format includes

- at least one driving question for each activity, to provide the initial engagement for the students and open the potential for inquiry;

- a list of materials needed for the activity (including resources on how to make or find the materials);

- the procedure for each activity; and

- a "Think About" section with open-ended questions that link directly to the driving question(s) and promote further student inquiry.

Chapter 1 focuses on the topic of topography. We begin with map interpretation and then apply our understanding of the topic to the form and structure of the landscape through the use of topographic maps.

In Chapter 2 we describe concepts related to physical geography. We explore the physical geogra-

Teachers using sieves to study the composition of the sediment in a stream bed

phy of a local area within the context of the natural resources, biomes, and habitats found in that area. We also integrate into this chapter the concept of a watershed, with an emphasis on the interaction between living and nonliving things as teachers and students investigate their surroundings.

In Chapter 3 we turn our attention to water, an essential ingredient for life. The physical and chemical properties of water are discussed, as well as how these properties are important for sustaining biological organisms.

The focus of Chapter 4 is soil, and specifically the relationship between soil conditions and local flora. Students learn that an examination of the soil can tell much about the area under investigation and which plants (and therefore animal life) are likely to be found there.

In Chapter 5 we discuss energy and nutrients. We begin with the topic of light energy and the importance this has as the primary source of energy for biological organisms. Then we deal with essential nutrients and the role each has in sustaining life. The main idea here is to link an understanding of essential nutrients to the nutrient loading of an aquatic system and the negative impact that overloading can potentially have on a system.

Chapter 6 focuses on biodiversity, specifically the study of living organisms found within a terrestrial habitat such as a forest and an aquatic habitat such as a stream. By combining a study of the biotic nature of a system with the chemical analyses (abiotic) done in Chapter 5, a clearer picture of the health of a system is gained.

Our theme in Chapter 7 is action projects. Here we provide examples of teacher-constructed units and classroom-tested activities designed within the contexts of the content areas presented earlier. Our goal is to showcase actual teacher and student projects that have used field-based learning experiences and action projects.

Chapter 8, "Reflections on Implementation," provides vignettes from those involved in the implementation of active science learning. These real stories provide insight into the successes and challenges of engaging students in individual classrooms as well as entire schools in inquiry, project, and field-based learning experiences.

Finally, as science educators, we understand how difficult it is to feel that you always have to "reinvent the wheel" or design completely new and unique learning activities for your students. Through our partnerships over the years we have found a wealth of resources that are immediately accessible and usable to all of us. In fact, the U.S. Environmental Protection Agency, in its "Tips for

Developing Successful Grant Applications," notes that there are many excellent existing materials on environmental education and recommends using these materials rather than new curricula (U.S. EPA 2009). We encourage you to collaborate with colleagues and form partnerships with outside agencies that enable you to spend more time in the planning and construction of materials that are engaging and contextualized, so students can have more direct experiences with learning in the field.

References

Bartosh, O. 2003. Environmental education: Improving student achievement. MA thesis, Evergreen State College.

Chesapeake Bay Program. 2000. Chesapeake 2000. *http://archive.chesapeakebay.net/agreement.htm*

Duffin, M., A. Powers, G. Tremblay, and Program Evaluation and Educational Research (PEER) Associates. 2004. Place-Based Education Evaluation Collaborative (PEEC): Report on cross-program research and other program evaluation activities, 2003-2004. *www.peecworks.org/PEEC/PEEC_Reports/S0019440A-003A00C7*

Falco, E. H. 2004. Environment-based education: Improving attitudes and academics for adolescents. (Evaluation report for South Carolina Department of Education.) *www.seer.org/pages/research/Southcarolinafalco2004.pdf*

H.R. 3036—110th Congress. 2007. No Child Left Inside Act of 2008. *www.govtrack.us/congress/bill.xpd?bill=h110-3036&tab=summary*

Hungerford, H. R., and T. Volk. 1990. Changing learner behavior through environmental education. *Journal of Environmental Education* 21 (3): 8–21.

Students and teachers at Piney Ridge Elementary School in Sykesville, MD, working on a wetland restoration project on school grounds

Lieberman, G. A., and L. L. Hoody. 1998. Closing the achievement gap: Using the environment as an integrating context for learning, executive summary. San Diego, CA: State Education and Environment Roundtable.

Louv, R. 2005. *Last child in the woods: Saving our children from nature deficit disorder.* Chapel Hill, NC: Algonquin Books.

Maryland State Department of Education. 2007. Professional Development School. Assessment framework for Maryland. *www.marylandpublicschools.org/NR/ rdonlyres/75608A85-6909-4BE3-A4D8-* *D08C759D0A5A/14214/SAssessmentFrame- workRevisedAugust2007.pdf*

National Environmental Education Training Foundation (NEETF). 2000. *Environment- based education: Creating high performance schools and students.* Washington, DC: NEETF.

National Research Council (NRC). 1996. *National science education standards.* Washington, DC: National Academies Press. *www.nap.edu/html/nses/1.html#goals*

National Research Council (NRC) Committee on Science Learning, Kindergarten Through Eight Grade. 2007. *Taking*

science to school: Learning and teaching science in grades K-8, ed. R. A. Duschl, H. A. Schweingruber, and A. W. Shouse. Washington, DC: National Academies Press.

National Science Foundation (NSF). 2006. Teacher Professional Continuum (TPC). *www.nsf.gov/funding/pgm_summ.jsp?pims_id=12785*

Project Learning Tree. 2006. *Exploring environmental issues: Places we live.* Washington, DC: American Forest Foundation.

State Education and Environment Roundtable (SEER). 2000. *California Student Assessment Project: The effects of environment-based education on student achievement.* San Diego, CA: SEER.

Taylor, A. F., and F. E. Kuo. 2009. Children with attention deficits concentrate better after walk in the park. *Journal of Attention Disorders* 12: 402–409.

U.S. Environmental Protection Agency (U.S. EPA). 2009. Tips for developing successful grant applications. *www.epa.gov/enviroed/granttips.html*

Youth in horticulture. 2005. Special section, *Journal of Horticulture Technology* 15, no. 3.

Topography

How do we start the process of learning about our environment? One way is to begin observing and recording what we see in the environment to develop both a mental model and concrete map of the world around us. Having students go outside to their school campus, town park, or local recreation area is a way to accomplish this process. Students will develop observational skills and increase awareness as they begin to see what they pass by daily or did not notice before; this process opens up their minds to inquiry and an interest in their environment, whether it be rural, suburban, or inner city. Discovering their own "backyard" and how to develop mapping skills will assist in the process of learning their connection to the environment.

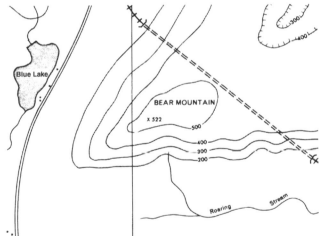

Map courtesy of Hubbard Division of American Educational Products, LLC

A Content Primer

This chapter introduces the topic of topography, including map use and interpretation, and then provides activities to help students apply their understanding of the topic to the form and structure of the actual landscape.

Definition

Topography is defined in *Merriam-Webster's Collegiate Dictionary, Eleventh Edition,* as "the configuration of a surface including its relief and the position of its natural and man-made features." *Topography*, therefore, refers to the relief of the land—for example, a steep versus a gentle hill—which can be represented by contour lines (lines of equal elevation) on a map. Such maps are called topographic maps.

A western river valley as photographed from approximately 30,000 feet

An Introduction to Maps

Interpreting maps is an excellent way to engage students in learning as they compare a model of their world (the map) to the real-life features found outside. Introducing children to maps need not be an arduous task, and students can begin the process of map interpretation by using local street maps and a simple map key (see example in Figure 1.1). During such an exploration we often hear students exclaiming "This is where I live!" or identifying other landmarks within the surrounding area.

Integrating map interpretation with technology is now easy to do. Using Google Earth 5

FIGURE 1.1
Examples of Map Symbols

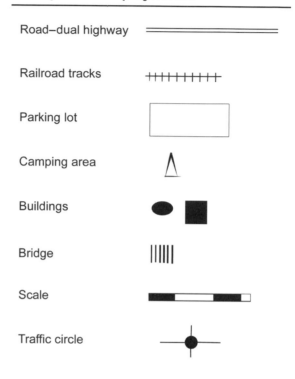

(*http://earth.google.com*) you can "visit" almost any location to view the landscape and identify actual landscape features, such as roads, rivers, streams with and without cover, housing developments, and agricultural areas. Now you and your students can see the direct relationship between map symbols and actual features.

Using Topographic Maps

We begin with topographic maps, used to discern the contour of the Earth's surface and useful for environmental studies, because they reveal a number of natural and human features that students will encounter in their studies. These maps provide a good framework for helping students build an understanding of the concept of a watershed (see Chapter 2). Topographic maps, also referred to as *contour maps,* are distinguishable

Topic: Topographic Maps

Go to: *www.scilinks.org*

Code: IO001

Topic: Mapping

Go to: *www.scilinks.org*

Code: IO002

FIGURE 1.2
A Comparison of Contour Lines (Values in Meters [m]) and Isobar Lines (Values in Millibars [mbars])

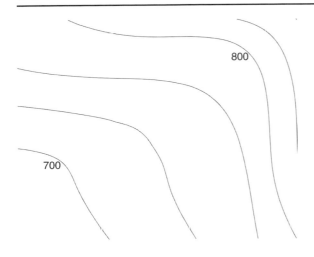

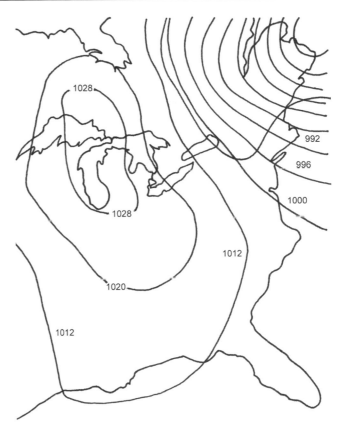

from street maps by the use of contour lines that represent changes in elevation. Similar to isobars of a weather map, which connect points of equal air pressure, contour lines connect points of equal elevation (see Figure 1.2). Thus, any point on a single contour line has the same elevation.

When looking at a contour map we also notice the distance between the lines. This distance represents how steep or gentle the landform is: The closer the lines, the steeper the land; the further apart, the gentler (Figure 1.3). The shaded area represents the steepest section between contours 700 and 800 meters.

Figure 1.4 (p. 4) is a simple model that shows how a contour map compares with the actual topography of the landform. In this example notice the steep hill on the left side of each diagram. The topographic map represents this steepness by the proximity of its lines: the closer the lines, the steeper the hill. Figure 1.4, part A, is part of an actual map and shows numerous landforms relative to the contour lines, especially steepness, and direction of stream flow into a

FIGURE 1.3
Contour Map With Shaded Area Representing Steepest Section of Landform

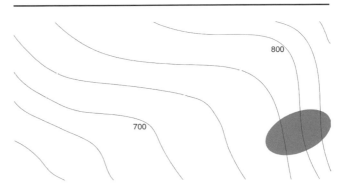

SCI LINKS.
THE WORLD'S A CLICK AWAY

Topic: Weather Maps
Go to: www.scilinks.org
Code: IO003

Topic: Mapmaking
Go to: www.scilinks.org
Code: IO004

valley. Part B of Figure 1.4 illustrates a side view of the hill sloping toward the valley.

We introduce the concept of *slope*, or *gradient*, here because understanding the slope of the Earth's surface will allow you to predict the location of streams. For example, a local low point in elevation does not indicate stream location, but a local low point in elevation between two adjacent hills with the contours forming a V/U shape in an uphill direction indicates a preferred path for storm water runoff or a flowing stream (see part A of Figure 1.4). Using a topographic map to determine slope will allow you to determine likely stream locations. Stream study is a key element of outdoor exploration for students of this age.

Figure 1.5 is a contour map to be used in performing a sample calculation for gradient.

FIGURE 1.5
Contour Map for Sample Calculation of Gradient

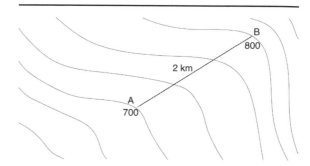

FIGURE 1.4
Model of a Hill on a Contour Map

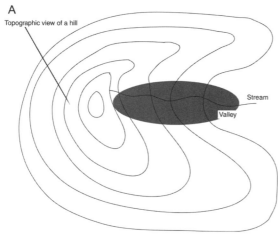

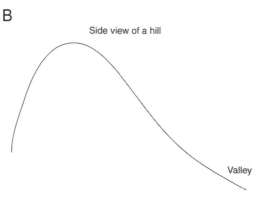

Formula and Sample Calculation for Gradient

Gradient is defined as the rate of change in the field value. Field value on a contour map is *elevation*. In other words, the gradient is the amount of change in elevation over a certain distance.

$$Gradient = \frac{change\ in\ elevation}{distance}$$

To calculate the gradient for Figure 1.5, first use a ruler to draw a straight line between points A and B. Record all values directly on your map. Record all elevations and distances and be sure to use proper units.

$$Gradient = \frac{800\ m - 700\ m}{2\ km}$$

$$Gradient = \frac{100\ m}{2\ km}$$

$$Gradient = 50\ m/km$$

Topography Activities

Activity 1. Geographic "Flights": An Exploration

Taking a trip to almost any location to view the landscape is now possible with the click of a mouse and the Google Earth 5 application. The mapped areas from this application make it easy to recognize roads, rivers, streams with and without cover, housing developments, agricultural areas, and so on. Try a few trips with the whole class to locations that are familiar to students and to places they would like to visit. Predicting what the landscape will look like prior to taking a "flight" can be a valuable exercise before students map their own backyard and will increase student awareness of the major features to consider in mapping.

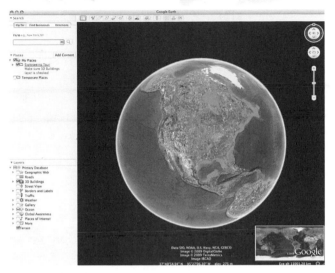

Google Earth screen capture

Driving Question

What becomes familiar as we view our location from above?

Materials

- Google Earth 5
  (*http://earth.google.com*)

- Computer and digital projector (helpful for displaying program to all students)

- Paper, pens, pencils, markers, rulers, and other illustrating tools for mapmaking

Procedure

Give students the following instructions:

1. Map a favorite place using Google Earth by using the "Fly To" search box in the upper-left corner of the window.

2. Once you arrive at the location use the zoom tool to move closer to or farther from the target. Note the various formations, colors, vegetation, water resources, buildings, and other features. Make a drawing using your best interpretation of what you see on the map and develop some symbols for what you see.

3. Now try this by flying to your school grounds. Draw a representation of what you see and then go outside the classroom and map the school campus and see if you can locate the features from the Google Earth map.

The maps that students draw will most likely vary from the overhead map because now they have a ground-level view of the location and will be able to see objects in greater detail within the immediate environment. The basic symbols shown in Figure 1.1 can be used as a guide for mapmaking, and students can make their own symbols to represent the features on their maps.

Think About

1. How does what you saw while "flying" compare with what you thought was actually on the ground?"

2. In what ways does "flying" help you identify landscapes?

Activity 2. Modeling a Contour Map

A simple means of constructing a model of a mountain is to use wooden ellipses of decreasing size and have students stack them from largest to smallest (like the ring-stacking activity that most young children have in their toy boxes) (Figure 1.6).

FIGURE 1.6
Wooden Model Used to Represent Change in Elevation of a Hill

Driving Question

How can we model contour lines using wooden ellipses?

Materials

- Wooden ellipses of different sizes; circles can also work. (These shapes are cut beforehand.)

- Diagram of topographic map (Figure 1.7)

- String or yarn

- Clear tape

Procedure

1. Have students stack ellipses (or circles) from largest to smallest.

2. Give students a topographic map of this wooden model so that they can see how the three-dimensional model is translated into a two-dimensional diagram (Figure 1.7). Using both the model and diagram reinforces the fundamental ideas that

- each contour line is separated from the adjacent contour line by the same elevation interval (i.e., the ellipses are the same height), and

- the different ellipses represent different total elevations (i.e., the top of the smallest ellipse is at a higher elevation than the top of the largest ellipse).

FIGURE 1.7
Two-Dimensional Diagram of Wooden Model in Figure 1.6

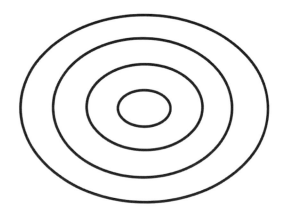

The next step in this process of understanding the relationship between contour lines and elevation is to show how the steepness of a landscape is directly related to how close or far apart contour lines are to each other on the map.

3. Returning to the wooden model, ask students to diagram a series of circles that represents what is shown in Figure 1.8. Use simple questions that prompt students to describe the

differences between the two sides and what this means for a real hill. Figure 1.9 shows the ideal student diagram, in which the left side represents a steep hill and the right side shows a gently sloping landscape.

FIGURE 1.8
Wooden Model of a Steep Hill

FIGURE 1.9
Ideal Student Diagram of Hill and Gentle Slope

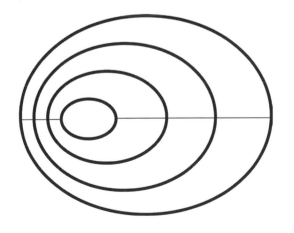

4. Use yarn to represent slope by taping a piece from the bottom of the left side to the top and doing the same on the right side and comparing the two.

Think About

1. What outside locations does this model resemble?

2. What is the difference in steepness represented by each piece of yarn?

3. How does the model of yarn translate to outside?

Activity 3. Creating a Simple Contour Map

As previously mentioned, one fundamental principle with contour maps is that contour lines connect points of equal elevation. Thus, any point on a single contour line has the same elevation.

Driving Question

What happens to elevation as you move along a single contour line?

Materials

• Paper with points and without contour lines (Figure 1.10, p. 8)

• Pencil

Procedure

1. To help students move beyond the idea in Activity 1 and better understand this concept, begin by giving them a scatterplot without lines (Figure 1.10) and ask them how they can determine the elevation of point A.

2. Referring back to the definition of a contour line, ask the students to draw lines on the paper that connect numbers of equal value (see Figure 1.11, p. 8). (In constructing this

simple contour map, students can gain an understanding that any two points on a line are sites of equal elevation and that they cannot determine the exact value at point A.)

3. Have students estimate the elevation at point A. (Based on the contours drawn, we can determine that point A's elevation is possibly between 24 and 32 meters.)

FIGURE 1.10
Scatterplot
(Numbers Represent Meters)

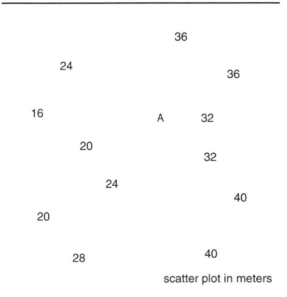

scatter plot in meters

Think About

1. What other lines on maps are similar to contour lines?

2. If you are walking along the water's edge at a lake, what happens to your elevation?

FIGURE 1.11
Scatterplot With Contour Lines

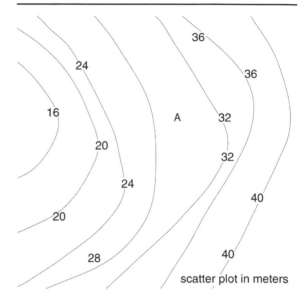

scatter plot in meters

Activity 4. Map Legends: An Exploration

The next step in the process of contour map use and interpretation is to have students review a relatively simple topographic map (Figure 1.12) and ask them to locate selected items. It is important for students to use a map's legend as an aid to help them decipher the various parts on the map. This activity serves well as an opportunity to reinforce concepts from social studies and encourage cross-curricular connections. Linking this activity directly to Activity 1 and Google Earth helps reinforce how features are represented on maps by using symbols.

For topographic maps the most important pieces of information on the legend are the contour intervals and the scale of the map. Figure 1.13 (p. 10) presents topographic map symbols published by the U.S. Geological Survey (USGS), a valuable resource for map use and interpretation (*http://edc2.usgs.gov/pubslists/booklets/symbols/ topomapsymbols.pdf*).

FIGURE 1.12
Bear Mountain Topographic Map

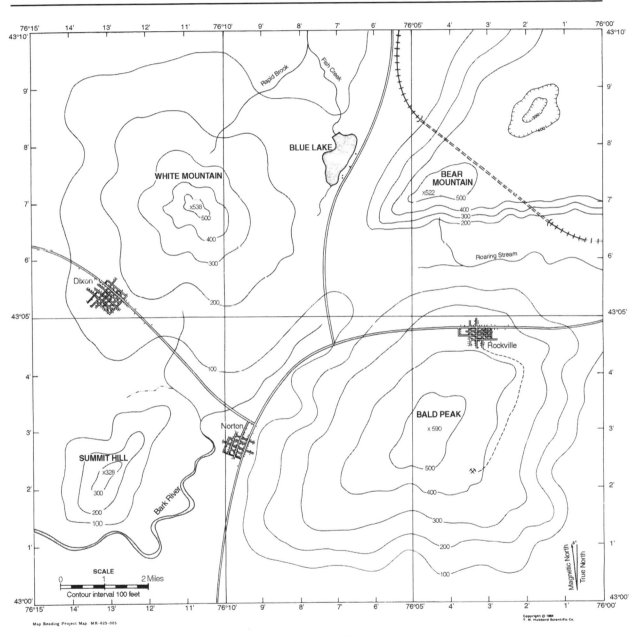

Map courtesy of Hubbard Division of American Educational Products, LLC

FIGURE 1.13
Symbols Used in USGS Topographic Maps

BATHYMETRIC FEATURES	
Area exposed at mean low tide; sounding datum line***	
Channel***	
Sunken rock***	

BOUNDARIES	
National	
State or territorial	
County or equivalent	
Civil township or equivalent	
Incorporated city or equivalent	
Federally administered park, reservation, or monument (external)	
Federally administered park, reservation, or monument (internal)	
State forest, park, reservation, or monument and large county park	
Forest Service administrative area*	
Forest Service ranger district*	
National Forest System land status, Forest Service lands*	
National Forest System land status, non-Forest Service lands*	
Small park (county or city)	

BUILDINGS AND RELATED FEATURES	
Building	
School; house of worship	
Athletic field	
Built-up area	
Forest headquarters*	
Ranger district office*	
Guard station or work center*	
Racetrack or raceway	
Airport, paved landing strip, runway, taxiway, or apron	
Unpaved landing strip	
Well (other than water), windmill or wind generator	
Tanks	
Covered reservoir	
Gaging station	
Located or landmark object (feature as labeled)	
Boat ramp or boat access*	
Roadside park or rest area	
Picnic area	
Campground	
Winter recreation area*	
Cemetery	Cem

COASTAL FEATURES	
Foreshore flat	Mud
Coral or rock reef	Reef
Rock, bare or awash; dangerous to navigation	
Group of rocks, bare or awash	
Exposed wreck	
Depth curve; sounding	
Breakwater, pier, jetty, or wharf	
Seawall	
Oil or gas well; platform	

CONTOURS	
Topographic	
Index	6000
Approximate or indefinite	
Intermediate	
Approximate or indefinite	
Supplementary	
Depression	
Cut	
Fill	
Continental divide	
Bathymetric	
Index***	
Intermediate***	
Index primary***	
Primary***	
Supplementary***	

CONTROL DATA AND MONUMENTS	
Principal point**	3-20
U.S. mineral or location monument	USMM 438
River mileage marker	Mile 69
Boundary monument	
Third-order or better elevation, with tablet	BM 9134 BM 277
Third-order or better elevation, recoverable mark, no tablet	5628
With number and elevation	67 4567
Horizontal control	
Third-order or better, permanent mark	Neace Neace
With third-order or better elevation	BM 52 Pike BM393
With checked spot elevation	1012
Coincident with found section corner	Cactus Cactus
Unmonumented**	

FIGURE 1.13 *(continued)*

CONTROL DATA AND MONUMENTS – *continued*

Vertical control

Third-order or better elevation, with tablet	BM ✕ 5280
Third-order or better elevation, recoverable mark, no tablet	✕ 528
Bench mark coincident with found section corner	BM + 5280
Spot elevation	✕ 7523

GLACIERS AND PERMANENT SNOWFIELDS

Contours and limits

Formlines

Glacial advance

Glacial retreat

LAND SURVEYS

Public land survey system

Range or Township line
  Location approximate
  Location doubtful
  Protracted
  Protracted (AK 1:63,360-scale)
  Range or Township labels R1E T2N
Section line
  Location approximate
  Location doubtful
  Protracted
  Protracted (AK 1:63,360-scale)
  Section numbers 1 - 36

Found section corner

Found closing corner

Witness corner WC

Meander corner MC

Weak corner*

Other land surveys

Range or Township line
Section line
Land grant, mining claim, donation land claim, or tract
Land grant, homestead, mineral, or other special survey monument
Fence or field lines

MARINE SHORELINES

Shoreline
Apparent (edge of vegetation)***
Indefinite or unsurveyed

MINES AND CAVES

Quarry or open pit mine	✕
Gravel, sand, clay, or borrow pit	✕
Mine tunnel or cave entrance	⊣
Mine shaft	▪
Prospect	X
Tailings	Tailings
Mine dump	
Former disposal site or mine	

PROJECTION AND GRIDS

Neatline	39°15' 90°37'30"
Graticule tick	55'
Graticule intersection	
Datum shift tick	

State plane coordinate systems

Primary zone tick	640 000 FEET
Secondary zone tick	247 500 METERS
Tertiary zone tick	260 000 FEET
Quaternary zone tick	98 500 METERS
Quintary zone tick	320 000 FEET

Universal transverse metcator grid

UTM grid (full grid)	273
UTM grid ticks*	269

RAILROADS AND RELATED FEATURES

Standard guage railroad, single track
Standard guage railroad, multiple track
Narrow guage railroad, single track
Narrow guage railroad, multiple track

Railroad siding
Railroad in highway
Railroad in road
Railroad in light duty road*

Railroad underpass; overpass

Railroad bridge; drawbridge

Railroad tunnel

Railroad yard

Railroad turntable; roundhouse

RIVERS, LAKES, AND CANALS

Perennial stream
Perennial river
Intermittent stream

Intermittent river

Disappearing stream
Falls, small
Falls, large
Rapids, small
Rapids, large

Masonry dam

Dam with lock

Dam carrying road

FIGURE 1.13 *(continued)*

RIVERS, LAKES, AND CANALS – *continued*	
Perennial lake/pond	
Intermittent lake/pond	
Dry lake/pond	Dry Lake
Narrow wash	
Wide wash	Wash
Canal, flume, or aqueduct with lock	
Elevated aqueduct, flume, or conduit	
Aqueduct tunnel	
Water well, geyser, fumarole, or mud pot	
Spring or seep	

ROADS AND RELATED FEATURES

Please note: Roads on Provisional-edition maps are not classified as primary, secondary, or light duty. These roads are all classified as improved roads and are symbolized the same as light duty roads.

Primary highway	
Secondary highway	
Light duty road Light duty road, paved* Light duty road, gravel* Light duty road, dirt* Light duty road, unspecified*	
Unimproved road Unimproved road*	
4WD road 4WD road*	
Trail	
Highway or road with median strip	
Highway or road under construction	Under Const
Highway or road underpass; overpass	
Highway or road bridge; drawbridge	
Highway or road tunnel	
Road block, berm, or barrier*	
Gate on road*	
Trailhead*	TH

SUBMERGED AREAS AND BOGS	
Marsh or swamp	
Submerged marsh or swamp	
Wooded marsh or swamp	
Submerged wooded marsh or swamp	
Land subject to inundation	Max Pool 431

SURFACE FEATURES	
Levee	Levee
Sand or mud	Sand
Disturbed surface	
Gravel beach or glacial moraine	Gravel
Tailings pond	Tailings Pond

TRANSMISSION LINES AND PIPELINES	
Power transmission line; pole; tower	
Telephone line	Telephone
Aboveground pipeline	
Underground pipeline	Pipeline

VEGETATION	
Woodland	
Shrubland	
Orchard	
Vineyard	
Mangrove	Mangrove

* USGS-USDA Forest Service Single-Edition Quadrangle maps only.

In August 1993, the U.S. Geological Survey and the U.S. Department of Agriculture's Forest Service signed an Interagency Agreement to begin a single-edition joint mapping program. This agreement established the coordination for producing and maintaining single-edition primary series topographic maps for quadrangles containing National Forest System lands. The joint mapping program eliminates duplication of effort by the agencies and results in a more frequent revision cycle for quadrangles containing National Forests. Maps are revised on the basis of jointly developed standards and contain normal features mapped by the USGS, as well as additional features required for efficient management of National Forest System lands. Single-edition maps look slightly different but meet the content, accuracy, and quality criteria of other USGS products.

** Provisional-Edition maps only.

Provisional-edition maps were established to expedite completion of the remaining large-scale topographic quadrangles of the conterminous United States. They contain essentially the same level of information as the standard series maps. This series can be easily recognized by the title "Provisional Edition" in the lower right-hand corner.

*** Topographic Bathymetric maps only.

Topographic Map Information

For more information about topographic maps produced by the USGS, please call: 1-888-ASK-USGS or visit us at http://ask.usgs.gov/

Source: U.S. Geologic Survey, *http://egsc.usgs.gov/isb/pubs/booklets/symbols*

Driving Question

What map symbols are used to represent real landforms?

Materials

- Contour map of Bear Mountain (Figure 1.12, p. 9)
- Copy of USGS topographic map symbols (Figure 1.13, p. 10)

Procedure

Have students find as many map symbols as they can.

Think About

What symbols did you find, and which ones represent features in your neighborhood?

Activity 5. Contour Lines: Part I

This is the first of two activities using the Bear Mountain map (Figure 1.12, p. 9) that can be modified to fit a selected grade. For example, while fifth-grade students and older may be able to determine the locations at a particular longitude and latitude, third-grade students may not be asked to do this. Instead, we may simply ask younger students to determine the contour interval and the elevation of particular locations on the map.

Introduction for Students

In this activity you will become familiar with contour lines and how to estimate elevation on a contour map. Record all elevations directly on the map.

Driving Question

What can contour lines tell us about landforms?

Materials

- Bear Mountain map (Figure 1.12)
- Ruler
- Pencil

Terms to Consider

- Contour line
- Contour interval
- Longitude and latitude
- Slope or gradient

Procedure

Give students the following instructions:

1. Determine the contour interval.

2. Determine the amount of latitude and longitude on this map.

3. Locate and determine the elevation for each of the following points.

   a. Norton

   b. Dixon

   c. Rockville

   d. Blue Lake

   e. Intersection of Fish Creek and Rapid Brook

   f. lat 43°05' N, long 76°10' W

   g. lat 43°09' N, long 76°11' W

   h. lat 43°08'30" N, long 76°02' W

   i. lat 43°06' N, long 76°03' W

   j. lat 43°04' N, long 76°11' 30" W

k. The point 2 miles due south of the mine on Bald Peak

l. The point 1.5 miles NE of the X on Summit Hill

Think About

1. What happens to the elevation as you walk along one contour line?

2. Which side of Bear Mountain is the steepest? How do you know?

3. How would you describe the land between Summit Hill and Norton?

4. Imagine you are walking north along the eastern shore of Blue Lake. Explain if you would be walking uphill or downhill. Verify your answer by "flying" to the shore of Lake Tahoe, Nevada. Zoom in so that you can clearly see the shoreline and the boat docks on the lake. Place the cursor (hand) along different parts of the shoreline and see what happens.

5. Identify one real-life situation you may encounter where you think it might be useful to have a contour map.

Activity 6. Contour Lines: Part II
Introduction for Students
You will determine the gradient of several lines on the map. Record all elevations directly on the map.

Driving Questions
1. How can we determine the gradient between two points on a contour map?

2. What does gradient tell us about physical geography of a locale?

Materials
• Bear Mountain map (Figure 1.12, p. 9)

• Ruler

• Pencil

Procedure
Give students the following information and instructions:

1. *Gradient* is defined as the rate of change in the field value. Field value on a contour map is *elevation*. In other words, the gradient is the amount of change in elevation over a certain distance.

$$Gradient = \frac{change\ in\ elevation}{distance}$$

2. Use a ruler to draw a straight line between the two points, and record all values directly on your map. Record all elevations and distances; be sure to use proper units.

3. Determine gradient for the following lines:

   a. Blue Lake to Bear Mountain

   b. Bald Peak to Bear Mountain

   c. Dixon to White Mountain

   d. Bald Peak to Rockville

   e. Summit Hill to White Mountain

Think About
Based on the latitude and longitude, where is Bear Mountain located?

Activity 7. Mapping the Schoolyard
Using maps is fun, but the impact of map use on student learning is diminished if students do not go outside and compare and contrast what

is on the map with what they see. The purpose of this activity is to extend student understanding of maps by having them go outside and create a map of their own school grounds. In fact, constructing a map of a study site can be foundational in beginning observations and investigations of a particular area.

Driving Question

What information about our school site can we convey on a map?

Materials

- Clipboard or some other hard surface, such as a book, to write on (if available)

- Pencil

- Blank paper

- Magnetic compass (available from any science education supplier)

Procedure

Pick a site outside that is at least 100 × 100 ft., and give students the following instructions:

1. Notice any and all objects in your site. Create a list and a key for each object (see examples of typical map symbols in Figure 1.1, p. 2).

Towson University preservice intern illustrating study site

2. Construct your schoolyard map. Be sure to use the compass to ensure directionality, and include the compass rose on your map.

Think About

Describe your site. Do you have a lot of open space, buildings, or a mixture? How could you make your site friendlier to plants and animals?

Activity 8. Constructing a Topographic Map Outside the Classroom[1]

The purpose of this activity is to directly involve students in the process of constructing real-scale contour lines on a real hill. The first step regarding preparation involves the selection of a hill that is best suited for this task. Select a hill with a low slope at the bottom and a steep slope at the top (see Figure 1.14 as an example) that is wide enough to accommodate your class size (about 40 ft. wide for a class of 24 students). Make sure that the spaces in which the students would work are not so steep that they present a safety hazard.

FIGURE 1.14
Side View of Hill

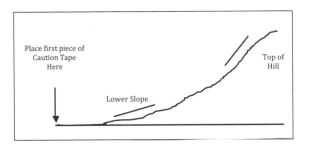

1   This activity was written and conducted with third-grade students by Pamela Lottero-Perdue, PhD, Assistant Professor of Science Education, and Steven Lev, PhD, Associate Professor of Geology, both of the Physics, Astronomy and Geosciences Department at Towson University.

When this study was conducted by Drs. Lottero-Perdue and Lev, about a 2 ft. elevation interval (contour interval) seemed appropriate and determined the best location for the first contour line. If, however, a 2 ft. elevation interval is not convenient, use the following method for changing the interval:

1. Determine the total height of the hill.

2. Determine the number of contour lines you would like the students to produce.

3. Divide the total height of the hill by the number of contour lines you would like your students to produce for their map. Here is a sample calculation if the hill is 40 ft. high and there are eight contour lines:

$$\text{Contour interval (CI)} = \frac{\text{height of hill}}{\text{number of contour lines}}$$

$$\text{CI} = \frac{40 \text{ ft.}}{8 \text{ lines}}$$

$$\text{CI} = 5 \text{ ft./line}$$

Instead of making a map with 2 ft. intervals, the students in this case would have a 5 ft. difference in elevation between each line.

The fundamental principles to learn from this activity are as follows:

- A topographic map is a map that shows the shape of the land surface.

- All points on a contour line are at the same elevation.

- Adjacent contour lines are separated by a fixed interval representing changes in elevation.

- Contour lines that are closer together represent steeper slope of the land surface, and lines spread further apart denote a more gradual incline.

- Geologists and surveyors measure elevations in the field carefully using special tools.

- Topographic maps are "to scale"—that is, they use a key to represent distance (e.g., "1" on the map represents 1 ft. of real distance) between contour lines and elevation.

Driving Question

How do we construct real-scale contour lines on an existing hill?

Materials

(for four groups of students and one teacher modeling station, with many parents to help; materials available at most home improvement stores)

- A large, standard level (for teacher demonstration purposes only)

- Five line levels

FIGURE 1.15
Job Necklaces

- Five wooden stakes, each about 4 ft. tall, with 2 ft. marked from bottom and a bullseye level glued to the top of each

- Five long sections (20 ft.) of brightly colored nylon string

- Twenty utility marker flags (a utility marker flag is a thin metal rod with a plastic flag)

- Masking tape or clip (to hold string to the stake at the 2 ft. mark if necessary)

- Spool of caution tape to make contour lines

- Indelible-ink pen

- Five sets of job necklaces (laminated for repeated use) to indicate the following jobs for each team, plus the chaperones/teacher: stake holder, bullseye level watcher, string holder, line level watcher, and flag placer (Figure 1.15)

Safety Concerns

- Be sure that students are careful with the utility flags (they should push the utility flags gently in the ground; tell them not to poke the flags at anyone).

- Ask the stake holders to refrain from sliding their hands on the stakes, to avoid getting splinters.

FIGURE 1.17
Prepared Site for Contour Line

- Everyone should be careful walking up and down the incline to avoid twisting ankles or other injury; there should be no running.

Procedure
Pre-Activity
Before students arrive lay a 27 ft. length of caution tape along the ground at the bottom of the hill. This represents contour line 1, and all points along this line are at the same elevation. Spread the four utility marker flags evenly across the tape, and use the flags to pin the tape to the

FIGURE 1.16
Group Stations

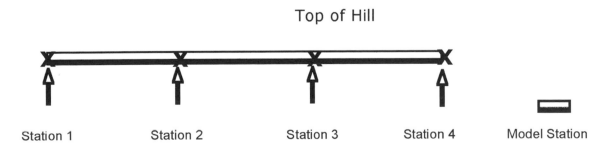

Top of Hill

Station 1   Station 2   Station 3   Station 4   Model Station

FIGURE 1.18
Students Standing Along Contour Line

ground. These four locations represent four group stations for the class (see Figure 1.16)

Place a bucket of tools for each group at each flag location. Each bucket should include a 4 ft. tall wooden stake, a line level, and a set of four utility marker flags. Prepare the stake as follows:

1. Mount a bullseye level flush with the top of the stake so that when the stake is perpendicular to a horizontal surface, the bullseye level is level.

2. Measure and mark 2 ft. of distance from the bottom of the stake with indelible ink.

3. Tie a 20 ft. length of nylon string to the stake at the 2 ft. mark, and then wrap the string around the stake.

Figure 1.17 (p. 17) shows the prepared site.

Implementation

1. Have the children line up along the first contour line (Figure 1.18). Explain that the task is to construct contour lines up the hill and that the difference in elevation between each contour line (or "interval") will be 2 ft.

2. Ask the children to think about where in the direction toward the top of the hill would be a point that is 2 ft. higher than where they are standing now. Ask them to walk to this point. (Predictions are usually wildly different; it appears difficult for the children to judge where this point would be.)

3. At the modeling station, begin the modeling process by holding up a simple carpenter's level to ask if any of the children have seen or used it. Next, show them the bullseye and line levels; make sure that each student is able to observe the levels up close. The basic principles of the modeling process are as follows:

- When the object being measured is horizontal, the bubble in the level is centered.

- The bullseye level is glued to the top of the stake to ensure that the stake is held perpendicular to the ground.

- The line level affixes to the string to ensure that the string is horizontal (or perpendicular to the force of gravity).

Continue the modeling process by demonstrating step by step how to determine the location of the next 2 ft. contour line from the starting point at contour line 1. As you model

FIGURE 1.19
Stake Holder

FIGURE 1.20
Line Level Watcher

the process, solicit the help of student volunteers and place the appropriate job necklace on each volunteer. The modeling process is as follows (job roles are in bold type):

a. Place the prepared stake at the contour line 1 location. The **stake holder** holds the stake (Figure 1.19) and works with the **bullseye level watcher** to ensure that the stake does not tilt. The bullseye level watcher ensures that the bubble remains in the center of the bullseye.

b. The **string holder** unfurls the string with the help of the stake holder and stretches it up the hill a few feet, pinning it to the ground with a thumb or finger while keeping the string taut.

c. The **line level watcher** places the line level on the taut string and communicates to the string holder whether or not the string is level (Figure 1.20). The string is level when the bubble remains in the center of the two lines on the line level. If it is not level, the string holder and

line level watcher need to work together to find where it is that the string holder must pin the string to the ground so that the taut string is level according to the line level. During this time, the bullseye level watcher and string placer must continuously ensure that the bottom of the stake is touching the ground and that it is not tilted.

d. Once the string holder and line level watcher have determined where the string must be pinned to the ground for the string to be level, the **flag placer** carefully places the utility marker flag in the ground at this location. This is the 2 ft. elevation location for contour line 2. This flag will remain in place until the end of this lesson—do not remove this flag!

e. Once the first 2 ft. elevation is determined, steps a through d are repeated, except the new starting point is not at the contour line 1 location, but rather at the

FIGURE 1.21
Going Uphill

FIGURE 1.22
Students Have Placed Utility Marker Flags for Contour Lines 2, 3, 4, and 5.

new contour line location indicated by the flag that was just placed.

   f. Repeat steps a through e to determine the locations of contour lines 3, 4, and 5. (Figure 1.21, p. 20).

4. Once steps a through f are completed and explained, ask children to get into their assigned groups and ask parent chaperones to split up across the groups. At least one parent per group is ideal.

5. Have each group work their way up the hill, placing flags at each subsequent 2 ft. elevation increase. Occasionally ask groups to predict where the next flag might be. (When Drs. Lottero-Perdue and Lev conducted this activity with third-grade children, the children got increasingly more accurate with their predictions, noting that the hill was getting steeper so the next contour line would be closer.) At each new contour line location, the children should switch job necklaces and corresponding tasks.

6. After all groups have successfully placed utility marker flags for contour lines 2, 3, 4, and 5 (see Figure 1.22), assign each group one set of flags (e.g., along contour line 2). Give each group a 30 ft. length of caution tape and ask them to stretch and pin it along the length of four utility marker flags. This is an exciting culmination of the groups' work, as the contour lines are striped across the hill quite visibly with the caution tape.

Notes on Implementation From Drs. Lottero-Perdue and Lev

A couple of adaptations may be necessary when you implement this activity. First, it may not be convenient for you to divide the hill into 2 ft.

elevation increments. If a different interval (e.g., 4 ft.) is better for your hill, simply change the length of and marking on the stake. Ultimately, dividing the total height of the hill by the number of contour lines you would like your students to produce for their map is the best way to settle on an appropriate contour interval. Do not wait until the day of the lesson to determine the best elevation interval of the hill. If possible, do the activity with a friend on the hill you have chosen prior to teaching this lesson to your students.

We strongly recommend parent chaperone assistance. In most cases, parents were quite helpful in organizing the switching of job necklaces and helping students navigate the steps of the process as the groups moved up the hill. If you have no or limited parent assistance, we recommend stopping all of the groups after each flag is placed along a particular contour line (e.g., for contour line 2), and having an explicit discussion in which students (1) compare the locations across groups, (2) predict where the next location may be, and (3) rotate job necklaces. To facilitate the rotation of jobs, ask each group to line up in order of their birthdays and have students give their job necklaces to the person on their right (or something similar); be sure that they stand in the same order each time this process is repeated. Conducting this lesson without parent assistance will take more time to conduct—perhaps 50 minutes instead of 25 minutes—but it can be done.

Think About

After the contour lines are striped across the hill, ask the children to walk carefully to the top of the hill, admire their work, and respond to the following questions (answers are in *italics*):

1. What is the difference in elevation between the first and second contour lines? *The second*

and third? The third and fourth? The fourth and fifth? *2 ft.*

2. If we assume that this bottom contour line is 40 ft. above sea level, then how much above sea level is the second contour line? *42 ft.* The third? *44 ft.*

3. Why are the contour lines close together in some places and far apart in others even when the elevation difference between adjacent contour lines is the same (2 ft.)? *When the ground is steeper, it doesn't take as much horizontal distance to increase elevation by 2 ft.; when the ground is less sloped, we have to walk a longer distance to get to 2 ft. of elevation.*

Wrap-Up

Understanding where we are located or attaining a "sense-of-place" (Project Learning Tree 2006) is a fundamental concept embedded within this chapter. Learning to use and interpret maps, especially topographic maps, integrates a number of content areas (geography, science, social studies, and mathematics) and allows students to visualize the concrete world in a more abstract, two-dimensional manner. For example, looking at a hill next to their school and then seeing how the topographic representation of the contour lines can characterize a real geographic feature is an important step in the critical-thinking process. Our intent is to have maps be but one tool for students to use as they move forward to investigate their outside world.

Resource List
Printed Material

Project Learning Tree. 2006. *Exploring environmental issues: Places we live.* Washington, DC: American Forest Foundation.

Websites

Google Earth 5

http://earth.google.com

U.S. Geological Survey Topographic Map
Symbols

*http://edc2.usgs.gov/publists/booklets/symbols/
topomapsymbols.pdf*

Physical Geography

2

Building on Chapter 1, physical geography becomes a way to identify and better understand the components in our environment and the structure of the landscape. Students will build on their observational skills and begin to use interpretation as a way to better understand the world around them. Discovering the value of various local habitats will give them a greater appreciation for the living and nonliving things in their world. For example, creating a wildflower garden (habitat) that attracts wildlife from insects to birds gives an immediate visual connection to the value of our natural resources and an easily accessible "field site" for the discovery of the connection between physical geography and the environment as a whole.

A Content Primer
Definitions
Physical geography "covers the topics relating to the surface of the earth—the landforms, glaciers, rivers, climate, oceans, earth-sun interaction, hazards, and more" (About.com, Physical Geography). These topics include what we see when we go outside: hills, fields, grass, trees, sidewalks, driveways, parking lots, streams, rivers, and any other physical feature we can describe.

In studying physical geography we believe that the terms *natural resources, biome,* and *habitat* are fundamental concepts in investigating the natural setting. We define *natural resources* as those components important to the environment. A *biome* is characterized by specific climate and geographic limits incorporating many habitats, with *habitat* simply being a specific place where a particular organism lives (see, e.g., the frog habitat in Figure 2.1, p. 24) within that biome.

Another important physical feature is a watershed, which directly ties a land area with all the water within its boundaries. The U.S. Environmental Protection Agency (EPA) defines a

Topic: What Is a Habitat?

Go to: *www.scilinks.org*

Code: IO005

Topic: Natural Resources

Go to: *www.scilinks.org*

Code: IO006

Topic: Biomes

Go to: *www.scilinks.org*

Code: IO007

**FIGURE 2.1
Frog Habitat**

w*atershed* as "the area of land where all the water that is under it or drains off it goes into the same place" (U.S. EPA).

Understanding these concepts will help in the investigation of your surroundings and allow for better understanding of the interaction of nonliving and living things.

Natural Resources, Biome, Habitat, and Watershed
Natural Resources

As you and your students move "inside-out" to investigate the natural setting of your schoolyard, one place to begin is with the distinction between renewable and nonrenewable resources. In the schoolyard maps that were created in Chapter 1, most of the items the students labeled were probably renewable resources such as trees, water, and soil. They may also have included nonrenewable items such as rocks, stones, and metal items (e.g., flagpoles and storm grates). Our purpose is not to create an exhaustive list of renewable and nonrenewable items but to identify those items that are natural or man-made and distinguish those that may have an impact (positive or negative) on the environment, such as litter, impervious surfaces (parking lots), recyclable items, and permanent structures. Ultimately, our focus is on the natural, physical features of our environment.

Biome

A biome, while a seemingly simple concept, can not only be divided into aquatic (fresh and marine) and terrestrial designations but also incorporate an integrated system of land and water. For example, the Amazon rain forest contains the Amazon River as well as terrestrial aspects, and the Chesapeake Bay is part of the temperate forest region of Maryland (Figure 2.2) and Virginia.

Within a geographic region a biome is determined by temperature and rainfall, which directly influence the dominant vegetation of that region. For example, a temperate deciduous forest biome has an average temperature of 50°F (hot summers and cold winters), with a moderate amount of rainfall (30–60 inches per year); this biome includes mainly trees and shrubs that shed their leaves during the winter months. Understanding these fundamental features of a biome allows us to identify the typical plants and animals within that biome.

Habitat

It is important to note that there can be many habitats in a particular biome. From the schoolyard maps, you and your students may have identified and illustrated habitats that exist on the school grounds (which is embedded within one biome). These habitats may have included forests, meadows and grasslands, ponds, streams, and any place where living things abound. The necessary

FIGURE 2.2
Gambrill State Park, Frederick County, MD

components of a habitat are those features that an organism needs to survive, including

- access to food and water,

- access to shelter, and

- its dependence on other physical factors (e.g., temperature, light, moisture).

For example, a millipede (Figure 2.3) may be found roaming on a forest floor in search of food and also finds shelter in the same location, which constitutes the millipede's habitat. An ant's habitat may consist of a well-defined area situated around its colony; this area may be relatively small but supplies the colony with food, water, and shelter. Many habitats may be found in one location, and our interest is in gaining a better understanding of how each habitat is defined for an individual organism.

FIGURE 2.3
Millipede

FIGURE 2.4
Example of Stream Order Within a Watershed

Watershed

Unlike a biome, which is determined by geographic boundaries and associated weather of that area, a watershed is strictly defined by its geography, with all of its water draining to one place. The Chesapeake Bay watershed, for example, is bounded geographically by six states in the mid-Atlantic region of the United States. This watershed can then be divided into smaller watershed areas that are specific to particular locales within the larger Chesapeake Bay. In other words, you can have small watersheds that together make up a larger watershed. One way to understand this concept is to look at the branching patterns of streams. In Figures 2.4 and 2.5, all streams leading to a single outlet (the number 4 on Figure 2.5) represent the larger watershed. The separate branching patterns are represented by numbers 1, 2, 3, etc.; these numbers refer to a system of classifying streams by size originally proposed by Strahler (1957).[1]

---

[1]   The numbers (orders) represent a hierarchy of the relative size of a stream, ranging from 1 (a perennial stream with no tributaries) to 12 (e.g., the Amazon River).

FIGURE 2.5
River System Sketch

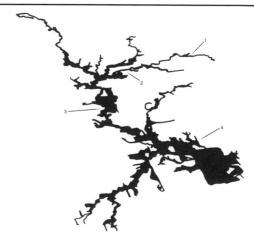

Another fundamental idea to understand about a watershed is that all water flows downhill to a common drainage point and that the topography is the determining factor of this flow. Therefore, as we look at the streams and rivers that make up a watershed we must also consider the associated landforms. Further investigation with Google Earth 5 reveals the relationship between landforms (physical geography) and their impact on the flow of water. We will learn more about this in Activity 2 in this chapter.

Riparian Buffers and Stream Structure

In this section we discuss the meaning and importance of two physical features, *riparian buffers* and *stream structure,* that directly relate to stream studies within a particular watershed.

Riparian Buffers

The word *riparian,* as defined in the *American Heritage Dictionary of the English Language, Fourth Edition* means "relating to the banks of a natural course of water." A riparian buffer is the natural vegetative cushion that mitigates or lessens the flow of runoff, nutrients, sediment, toxins, and other contaminants into the body of water. The limiting of runoff directly enhances water infiltration back into the aquifer (groundwater). In fact, properly "installed" buffers have been shown to remove 50% or more of nutrients and pesticides, 60% or more of certain pathogens, and 75% or more of sediment (U.S. Department of Agriculture, Natural Resources Conservation Service). Buffers also enhance wildlife habitat by providing cover and food sources, and for stream organisms buffers help reduce water temperature, which can reduce stress. Thus, assessing the physical structures surrounding a local body of water (stream, pond, or lake) can give a good representation of the quality of the overall habitat of this area. Habitat assessment is useful because "it may help answer questions about the benthic community based upon the habitat assessment score" (Stacey T. Brown, Virginia Save Our Streams, e-mail, April 12, 2006).

Figure 2.6 provides a model of the three-zone buffer system described by the Maryland Department of Natural Resources (DNR). In describing this system the Maryland DNR states that the ideal scenario has "all of the benefits that the forest has to offer; an effective buffer against non-point source pollution, habitat for fish and wildlife, areas for recreation, and a renewable source of forest products." Such benefits are outlined in Table 2.1 (p. 28). In Figure 2.7 (p. 29) a stream without a significant forest buffer is observed; this situation can lead to water quality problems.

Topic: Rivers and Streams

Go to: *www.scilinks.org*

Code: IO010

Topic: Water Properties

Go to: *www.scilinks.org*

Code: IO011

Topic: Water Pollution and Conservation

Go to: *www.scilinks.org*

Code: IO012

FIGURE 2.6
Three-Zone Buffer Model

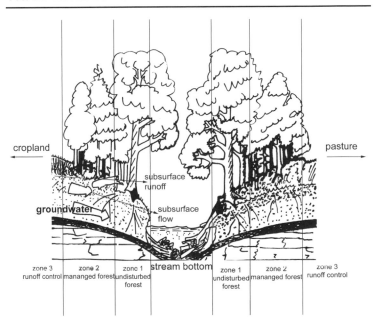

TABLE 2.1
Benefits of Three-Zone Riparian Buffer

Location of Buffer	Benefits
Zone 1: located directly on the stream or shore portion, stretching upland from the edge of the water	• Stabilizes the stream bank • Provides habitat for aquatic organisms • Trees and shrub roots "lock in" soil to resist erosion caused by flowing water. • Organism habitat and biodiversity increased by fallen logs, which slow stream flow and create pools that form unique "microenvironments" • Leaf canopy provides shade that controls water temperature and provides food sources for aquatic life. (Maximum summer temperatures of a nonforested stream may be 10–20°F warmer than a forested stream.)
Zone 2: located immediately upslope from zone 1	• Removes, transforms, or stores nutrients, sediments, and pollutants flowing over the land surface or in groundwater • Leaf, twig, and branch debris slows and traps sediments from runoff. This increases nutrients' infiltration into the ground, where they can be "used" by trees. (Up to 90% of nitrates can be removed by plant uptake.) • Can be a "managed forest" providing firewood and forest product
Zone 3: located immediately upslope of zone 2	• Grass filter strips or other control measures slow runoff, filter sediment and chemicals, and allow water to better infiltrate into the ground. • The buffer acts to spread out the flow of water and prevents excessive runoff from adjacent land uses. (Grass filter strips can remove 50% or more of sediment runoff and nutrients such as phosphorous.)

Source: Adapted from *www.dnr.state.md.us/forests/publications/sink.html*

FIGURE 2.7
Example of a Stream Without a Significant Forest Buffer

Stream Structure

The next step in habitat assessment deals directly with the stream itself. Streams can be characterized in three ways relative to their channel structure: straight, meandering, or braided. The type of channel of a stream relates directly to the stream's water flow, which then affects the variety of features embedded within the stream (Figure 2.8).

Figure 2.9 (p. 30) is a photo taken from 30,000 ft. that shows an obvious meandering pattern established by a river. Within any stream there may be several typical features:

- A cut bank (generally the outer edge of meander)

FIGURE 2.8
Stream Structure

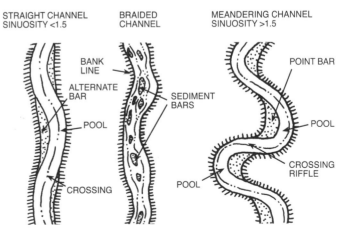

Citation and permission from Ohio DNR.
Source: Ohio Stream Management Guide 3: Natural Stream Processes, Ohio Department of Natural Resources. *www.dnr.state.oh.us/tabid/4159/default.aspx*

FIGURE 2.9
Example of Meandering Pattern

- A pool (generally the middle to inner edge of a meander)

- A point bar (generally inside a meander and an area of slowing water where deposition occurs)

- A riffle (generally a straight, shallow, fast-moving section of water containing small rocks—see more detailed definition below)

For our purposes in this chapter we are looking for a stream that contains *riffles,* defined as stretches of shallow, relatively fast-moving water that contain stones ranging in size from large pebbles (0.2–6.4 cm diameter) to cobbles (6.4–25.6 cm in diameter) (New York State Earth Science Regents Reference Tables). Stones of these sizes are excellent attachment sites for a variety of macroinvertebrates, and students can conduct biological sampling to assess the overall well-being of the stream (see Chapter 6, Biodiversity, p. 111). An ideal riffle is two times the width of the stream and maintains its width across the entire stream (Figure 2.10). The stream in Figure 2.11 illustrates characteristics of a riffle—shallow, fast moving, and fairly uninterrupted.

FIGURE 2.10
Riffle Diagram

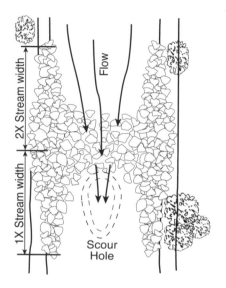

Plan View

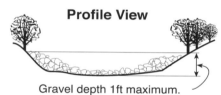

Profile View

Gravel depth 1ft maximum.

Citation and permission from Ohio DNR.
Source: Ohio Stream Management Guide 3: Natural Stream Processes, Ohio Department of Natural Resources. *www.dnr. state.oh.us/tabid/4159/default.aspx*

FIGURE 2.11
Characteristic Riffle

Additional physical characteristics of a stream to look for are

- alterations to the channel (generally human) that affect flow;

- bank conditions (highly eroded, steep or shallow, and/or natural or human influences);

- conditions of the stream (what is in the stream?), including embeddedness (generally referring to immobile rocks, fallen trees, or other material) and sedimentation of material (these conditions relate to size and immovability of materials such as rocks and trees); and

- attachment sites for invertebrates—these sites are linked to conditions of the stream and also provide fish shelter and shade, which in turn are linked to buffers.

Topography is of special importance to sampling stream riffles because stream gradient determines stream flow and, thus, whether the proper conditions for riffles will be found. Therefore, the emphasis on geography and map interpretation is an excellent means of content integration into the study of the environment. The integration of topography and physical geography is useful in habitat analysis as students assess the physical characteristics and quality of the surrounding stream buffer. In doing so students are able to analyze the potential and actual impact that the local community may have on the stream site.

Physical Geography Activities

In this section we provide activities that allow students to assess the physical habitat of their immediate schoolyard and then extend this inquiry toward a stream habitat analysis. Ideally, the stream study will be included within the watershed of the school with an apparent link between the schoolyard habitat and surrounding watershed. The activities can be adapted to a variety of settings using materials from local, regional, state, and national environmental organizations (e.g., Maryland DNR, the Izaak Walton League, the Chesapeake Bay Foundation, Virginia Save Our Streams, and the EPA).

Activity 1. What Is Your Watershed Address?

This activity encourages students to recognize and explore their watershed by using state or regional road maps that cover enough area to incorporate many rivers and streams. Have students first identify their immediate location and then find and trace all streams (including creeks and rivers) that flow or lead directly into a larger body of water. Have them trace these streams as far back (upstream) as they can. Next have them trace the outer boundary that includes all of these streams. This outer boundary represents their watershed.

For example, in our locale (Baltimore, Maryland) we used a regional road map that included the following states: New York, Pennsylvania, New Jersey, Maryland, Delaware, Virginia, and West Virginia. Students marked Baltimore as their location and then, using a blue highlighter, traced all streams and rivers that flowed into the Chesapeake Bay. Using a green marker they then traced the outer boundary of the streams and rivers. The intent was to show them how the Chesapeake Bay receives water from all of these sources and thus is the major watershed of the area.

Driving Questions

1. What does it mean to be part of a watershed?

2. Based on where I live, how would my watershed be defined?

Materials

- State or regional road map

- Highlighters or dry erase markers (black, blue, green, and red; use only low- or non-VOC markers)

Procedure

Have students use the road maps and highlighters or markers as follows:

1. Ask them to use *black* to mark on the map where they are located.

2. Ask them to use *blue* to trace all water (rivers, streams, etc.) that flows into the main body of water.

3. Ask them to use *green* to trace the outer boundary of all water flowing into the bay.

4. Have a class discussion in which students compare their boundaries (green lines) to the boundary of the actual watershed.

5. If the actual watershed boundary is different from their boundaries, ask the students to use *red* to trace the correct boundary.

Think About

1. In what direction does water always flow?

2. What does the previous answer tell you about the elevation of river sources?

3. What are the main rivers flowing into your body of water?

4. What are the smaller rivers that flow into these larger ones?

5. What does the pattern of flowing rivers remind you of?

6. What is a watershed?

7. What is our watershed?

8. Where are we located in our watershed?

Activity 2. Go With the Flow: An Exploration

This activity is a variation on Activity 1 using Google Earth 5; it is an excellent exercise for students and teachers to make connections to our "digital" landscape. There are any number of activities that can be generated with Google Earth 5 to promote student inquiry; this is but one example of the simple investigations that can be done with this interactive tool.

Driving Question

Why does the Mississippi River flow from Minneapolis, Minnesota, to the Gulf Coast of the United States?

Materials

• Google Earth 5 (*http://earth.google.com*)

• Computer and digital projector (helpful for displaying program to all students)

Procedure

Give students the following instructions and questions:

1. "Fly" to Minneapolis, Minnesota, and find the Mississippi River near Nicollet Island. At the bottom of the Google Earth window you will see a display of the latitude, longitude, and elevation (above sea level) as the cursor (hand) is moved from place to place. You'll see that at this location the elevation is 243 meters (m) above sea level. What does "above sea level" mean?

2. Go to the East Coast. How about Ocean City, Maryland? Place the cursor in the surf in Ocean City and you'll see the elevation is 0, as expected. So our land feature elevation is based on its relationship to sea level (coastal area), which is recorded as 0.

3. Now go to Memphis, Tennessee, and find the Mississippi River. After zooming in, place the cursor in the middle of the river and note the elevation—61 m. What happened?

   Lastly, fly to New Orleans, Louisiana, and note the elevation of 3 m. Wow!

Think About

1. What does this activity prove about the flow of water from one location to another?

2. Test your idea from the first question by completing "Go With the Flow" with a local river or stream. How do the results compare with those from the Mississippi River?

Activity 3. Schoolyard Habitat Assessment

In our first habitat assessment activity we use the Chesapeake Bay Foundation's Schoolyard Report Card data sheet (see Appendix A at the end of this chapter) as the basis for student inquiry into the schoolyard. Here students gain an initial experience in essential science process skills of observation and analysis. The goal is to determine the relative quality of the schoolyard habitat and to generate potential solutions to problems. These solutions then form the foundation for habitat action projects that are presented in Chapter 7.

If your school is not in the Chesapeake Bay area, you can modify the third driving question and the Schoolyard Report Card to reflect your area.

Driving Questions

1. What are the major factors to consider in determining the health of my schoolyard habitat?

2. How is my schoolyard doing?

3. Is my schoolyard helping the Chesapeake Bay or contributing to the Bay's current problems?

Materials

- Schoolyard Report Card (Appendix A; one copy per group)

- Schoolyard area to evaluate

Procedure

Place students into groups and give each group a copy of the Schoolyard Report Card. Each group should survey the area to fill out the report card.

Think About

What factor or events had the largest impact on your score?

Activity 4. At-Home Habitat Assessment

This activity allows students to apply their understanding of habitat assessment to the outdoor surroundings of their own home. Teachers should communicate with parents and guardians to involve them in supervising this activity. Also, be aware that home yards treated with pesticides and other hazardous chemicals should be avoided.

Driving Question

How does the health of the environment surrounding my home compare with my schoolyard habitat?

Materials

- Your Yard Report Card data sheet (Appendix B)

Procedure

Hand out the Your Yard Report Card to students and ask them to fill it out at home.

Think About

1. What does your score indicate about the environment surrounding your home?

2. What do you believe were some of the major factors contributing to this score?

3. What is one thing that you could do to increase your score?

Activity 5. Stream Habitat Assessment

Earlier in this chapter we introduced the concepts of a riparian buffer, stream morphology, and the conditions for an ideal riffle. Our next inquiry activity focuses on the habitat assessment of a nearby stream. If the school does not have an adjacent stream we suggest using a local site that is easily reached for a day trip. Teachers should visit the location to review any potential safety issues in advance of the trip with students.

The stream habitat assessment begins with the observation and documentation of the immediate physical surroundings, particularly the riparian buffer. This activity asks students to apply their conceptual understanding to a field study of a stream habitat. Students should fill out stream habitat assessment forms, which you can obtain from Virginia Save Our Streams at *www.vasos.org/pages/downloads.htm* (PDF location: *www.vasos.org/SOS_Revised%20Habitat%20 Form%20-%20HighGradientmay2007.pdf*).

Driving Questions

1. How do we determine the health of a stream habitat?

2. How does the health of our local stream compare with the health of the other habitats we have studied?

Materials

- Stream site with sufficient space for all groups
- Stream habitat assessment forms (*www.vasos. org/pages/downloads.htm* or *www.vasos.org/ SOS_Revised%20Habitat%20Form%20-%20 HighGradientmay2007.pdf*)

Procedure

Give students the following instructions:

1. Find the 100 m section of the stream assigned to you by your teacher. You may find it help-

ful to split the 100 m up into smaller sections while you work. Make sure you know where your section begins and ends.

2. Make sure you know the 10 habitat categories that you will be looking at when you collect data.

3. Walk or otherwise observe the entire 100 m stretch to be studied. You may find it helpful to sketch your site on the graph paper provided, making note of the riffle areas, pools, runs, glides, and other features such as log-jams or debris.

4. Refer back to Chapter 1, Activity 7 (Mapping the Schoolyard, p. 14). Construct a map of

FIGURE 2.12
Example of a Study Site Map

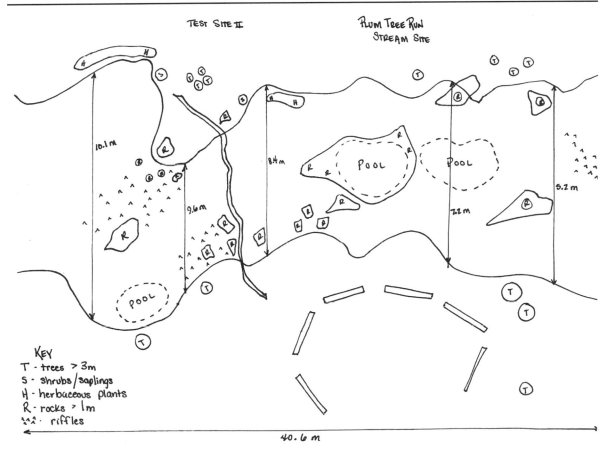

KEY
T - trees > 3m
S - shrubs/saplings
H - herbaceous plants
R - rocks > 1m
⋰⋰ - riffles

FIGURE 2.13
Example of a Stream Drawing

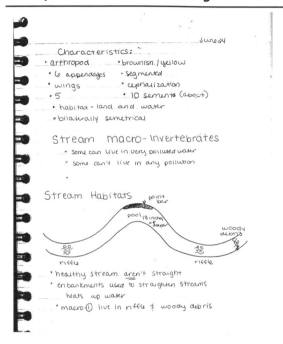

your study site (see Figures 2.12 and Figure 2.13, pp. 35–36, for examples).

5. Begin collecting your data using questions from the stream habitat assessment forms.

6. Add all of the subscores together to get a final score at the end of the data sheet.

Think About

1. What factor do you think was most influential in the score your stream received?

2. How does the health of your stream habitat compare with the health of your schoolyard habitat? Explain any similarities or differences.

3. What is the most important thing you think could be done to improve the score of your local stream habitat?

Wrap-Up

The preceding activities, while initially in the form of explorations, lay the foundation for the remainder of our *Inside-Out* field studies. The intent is not only for students to assess the initial quality of their surroundings but, more important, to begin asking questions about how to improve the studied habitats. It is these questions that are the beginning of action projects where students initiate additional investigations and propose solutions to better the world around them.

Resource List
Printed Material

Strahler, A. N. 1957. Quantitative analysis of watershed geomorphology. *Transactions of the American Geophysical Union* 38: 913–920.

Websites

About.com, Physical Geography
http://geography.about.com/od/physicalgeography/ Physical_Geography.htm

Chesapeake Bay Foundation
www.cbf.org

Izaak Walton League
www.iwla.org

Maryland Department of Natural Resources ("About Forest Buffers...")
www.dnr.state.md.us/forests/publications/sink.html

New York State Science Reference Tables, 2001 Earth Science, Revised November 2006 (p. 6)
www.nysedregents.org/testing/reftable/reftable.html

U.S. Department of Agriculture, Natural Resources Conservation Service ("Buffer Strips: Common Sense Conservation")
www.nrcs.usda.gov/feature/buffers/#Anchor-WhatBuffer

U.S. Environmental Protection Agency
www.epa.gov; www.epa.gov/nps/nps_edu/ whatx5.html (stream ordering activity); *www. epa.gov/owow/watershed/whatis.html*

Virginia Save Our Streams
www.vasos.org/index.htm

Appendix A

Schoolyard Report Card

Source: Adapted from Chesapeake Bay Foundation, *www.cbf.org/Document.Doc?id=95*

Runoff/Erosion
1. After looking at your schoolyard map describe where in this range it falls. 1 2 3 4 5 6 7 8 9 10 (1 = entirely made of concrete) (10 = totally forested)
2. Your school roof drains rainwater into mostly: a. well-vegetated trees and shrubs or unmowed grass (10 pts) b. mowed grass (5 pts) c. bare soil or impervious surface (4 pts) d. directly into storm drain (0 pts) e. even mix of all (5 pts)
3. Look for patches of bare soil and signs of erosion such as areas where rainwater has carved out ditches or washed out vegetation. The schoolyard has: a. very little erosion and few patches of bare soil (10 pts) b. several patches of bare soil or areas where soil is eroding (7 pts) c. mostly bare, exposed soil or impervious surfaces (0 pts)
4. Does your school have any of these runoff control systems: Rain garden ....2 pts Rain barrel ....2 pts Meadow ....2 pts Wetland ....2 pts Forested buffer zone (More than 50 feet wide)..2 pts
Your Score **Runoff/Erosion Total** _____

Appendix A (*continued*)

Transportation

1. **Determine the number of people employed at your school (teachers, maintenance staff, food service staff, administrators, etc.) by asking office staff. Look at the school parking lot and determine the number of vehicles relative to the number of employees.**
   a. There are 50% fewer cars in the parking lot than employees. (10 pts)
   b. There are 25% fewer cars in the parking lot than employees. (7 pts)
   c. There is about one car per employee in the parking lot. (5 pts)

2. **Are there bicycle racks at your school and do people use them?**
   a. The bike rack is full of bikes. (10 pts)
   b. The school has a bike rack but there are only a few bikes in it. (7 pts)
   c. The school has no bike rack and no bikes on the property. (0 pts)

3. **Is there any reward or encouragement for teachers or students who walk to school, ride their bikes, carpool, or take public transit?**
   a. Yes (10 pts)
   b. No (2 pts)

4. **Where does rainwater drain after hitting the parking lot?**
   a. highly vegetated area (10 pts)
   b. mowed or slightly vegetated drainage ditch (7 pts)
   c. storm drain marked "Chesapeake Bay Drainage"
   d. unmarked storm drain

Your Score Transportation Total _____

Appendix A (*continued*)

Vegetation

1. Describe the vegetation in your schoolyard:
   a. Trees and bushes cover a significant part of the schoolyard. (10 pts)
   b. Trees and bushes dot the landscape of the schoolyard. (6 pts)
   c. There are few or no trees in the schoolyard. (0 pts)

2. How much of the grass and vegetated areas in your school is being mowed?
   a. less than 50% (10 pts)
   b. between 50% and 80% (6 pts)
   c. more than 80% (4 pts)

3. Ask your school's lawn service or school maintenance staff how the mowed grass on the school grounds is fertilized.
   a. Grass clippings are left on the grounds as natural fertilizer. (10 pts)
   b. Lawn fertilizer is used according to a formula after doing soil tests. (8 pts)
   c. Lawn fertilizer is used according to instructions. (6 pts)
   d. Lawn fertilizer is applied randomly. (5 pts)

4. Describe the vegetation in the lowest lying part of your schoolyard:
   a. well vegetated with trees and shrubs (10 pts)
   b. vegetated with unmowed grass (8 pts)
   c. mowed grass (7 pts)
   d. bare soil, pavement, or concrete (0 pts)

Your Score **Vegetation Total** _____

Appendix A (*continued*)

Biodiversity

1. **By counting the different types of leaves or bark, how many different types of trees are there in your schoolyard?**
  a. 10 or more (10 pts)
  b. 7–9 (8 pts)
  c. 4–6 (5 pts)
  d. less than 4 (4 pts)

2. **By counting the different types of leaves and berries, how many different types of shrubs are there in your schoolyard?**
  a. 7 or more (10 pts)
  b. 4–6 (7 pts)
  c. less than 4 (4 pts)

3. **Below are examples of habitats for animals. Which of the following apply to your schoolyard?**
(4 pts for each)
  a. woodlands with many layers of plants and trees
  b. tall grassy fields or meadow
  c. thick brush and brambles or a brush pile
  d. dead standing trees or rotting logs on the ground
  e. streams with forested buffers

Your Score **Biodiversity Total** _____

****** BONUS ******
Awareness
1. **Does your school have an environmental club, offer environmental science classes, or include a bay unit in science class?** (1 pt for each yes) <div align="right">_____Total</div>
2. **Is there a stream in your schoolyard? Is there access?** (1 pt for each yes) <div align="right">_____ Total</div>

3. **Are there energy-saving devices?** (1 pt for each yes)
 	
  _____compact fluorescent
  _____skylights
  _____signs reminding you to turn off lights
<div align="right">_____ Total</div>

4. **Test your principal/administrator/science teacher:** (2 pts for each correct answer)
  a. Is there a body of water attached to your schoolyard?
  b. What is the closest sewage treatment plant?
  c. Where is the closest landfill?
  d. Is there incentive for the staff to use public transit? (2 pts for yes)
  e. Does your school recycle? (2 pts for yes)
  f. Do you want to improve your schoolyard? (2 pts for yes)
<div align="right">_____ Total</div>

Appendix A (*continued*)

Add Up Your Score and Find Out!

Now it's time to add your scores together to find out the health of your schoolyard.

Category	Points
Runoff/Erosion	
Transportation	
Vegetation	
Biodiversity	
Total	=
+ Bonus Points	+
Total + Bonus Points	=

Points	Grade	What Your Score Means
100–80	A–B	Your school is an excellent habitat for many plants and animals and is a very healthy part of the watershed!
79–60	C–D	You are on the right track, but there is more work to do.
59 or less	F	Poor habitat

Appendix B

Your Yard Report Card	Points

1. Downspouts. A downspout is a tube that delivers water from the roof to the ground. What type of surface receives the water from your home's downspout?
   a. Directly onto mulch or vegetation (2 pts)
   b. A path of rocks or a small concrete block (1 pt)
   c. Onto ground that is eroding (0 pts)
   d. Directly into storm water (0 pts)	

2. Erosion. Look for patches of bare soil, especially on a hillside.
   a. Very little erosion and bare patches or none at all (2 pts)
   b. Several patches of bare soil or areas where soil is eroding (1 pt)
   c. Large patches of bare soil and/or extensive erosion (0 pts)	

3. Pathways. Paths of heavily trafficked areas that cannot maintain vegetation.
   a. Covered with surface material that can filter and/or absorb water such as gravel, mulch, or wooden slats (2 pts)
   b. Covered with impervious material such as cement, asphalt, or bricks with mortar (1 pt)
   c. Bare, exposed soil (0 pts)	

4. Mowed Grass. How much of the yard is mowed grass?
   a. Less than 50% mowed (2 pts)
   b. Between 50% and 80% mowed (1 pt)
   c. More than 80% mowed (0 pts)	

5. Height of Mowed grass
   a. Grass is mowed 3–3½ inches. (2 pts)
   b. Grass is mowed 1½–2½ inches. (1 pt)
   c. Grass is mowed below 1½ inches. (0 pts)	

6. Grass Clippings
   a. Clippings are left on lawn to biodegrade and add nutrients. (2 pts)
   b. Clippings are bagged and dumped in compost pile. (1 pt)
   c. Clippings are bagged and sent to the landfill. (0 pts)	

7. Compaction. To test for compaction, see how far a screwdriver will sink into the ground.
   a. The screwdriver easily sinks all the way to the handle. (2 pts)
   b. The screwdriver sinks with some difficulty. (1 pt)
   c. The screwdriver is very difficult to sink into the ground and/or it will not sink at all. (0 pts)	

8. Mulch. How much mulch has been placed in gardens and around trees?
   a. 3+ inches of mulch (2 pts)
   b. 1–2 inches of mulch (1 pt)
   c. No mulch (0 pts)	

9. Weeds. How weedy is the lawn? For this measure, weeds are good! (To measure take a 5 m long string and place at a diagonal across the lawn. Count the number of weeds touching the string.)
   a. More than five weeds are touching the string or there are more weeds than grass. (2 pts)
   b. Between one and five weeds are touching the string or there is about half weeds and half grass. (1 pt)
   c. No weeds are touching the string or very few if any weeds are growing in the lawn. (0 pts)	

10. Earthworms. Dig in three sections of soil and also look for earthworm castings.
   a. Many earthworms and/or castings are found. (2 pts)
   b. Few earthworms and/or castings are found. (1 pt)
   c. No earthworms and/or castings are found. (0 pts)	

Appendix B (*continued*)

11. Fertilizer. What type, if any, of fertilizer is used?
    a. Natural compost is used and/or no fertilizer is used. (2 pts)
    b. Chemical fertilizer is used only once a year. (1 pt)
    c. Chemical fertilizer is used more than once a year. (0 pts)	

12. Native Plants. Are native plants used for landscaping?
    a. 20 or more native plants are visible around the yard. (2 pts)
    b. Fewer than 20 (but more than 0) native plants are seen in the yard. (1 pt)
    c. No native plants are seen in the yard. (0 pts)	

13. Compost Pile. A compost pile of grass clippings, leaves, or kitchen scraps is used.
    a. There is a compost pile in the yard. (2 pts)
    b. There is not a compost pile in the yard. (0 pts)	

14. Native Wildlife. Does the yard promote or support wildlife through the use of either native plants or bird feeders and bird boxes?
    a. The yard has native plants for hummingbirds and/or butterflies, bird boxes, and bird feeders. (2 pts)
    b. The yard has only a bird feeder. (1 pt)
    c. The yard has nothing to support native wildlife. (0 pts)	

Rain Barrel Bonus Points (1 per barrel)	
Your Score	

28–26 = extremely environmentally friendly yard	
25–22 = environmentally friendly yard	
21–18 = somewhat environmentally friendly yard	
17–14 = not too environmentally friendly yard	
0–13 = unfriendly to the environment	

3

Water

The same water that has existed on Earth for millions of years travels through a series of steps in a cycle from mountains to the sea, flows in and out of the cells in your body, and comprises 95% of the mass of a jellyfish. In short, water is the connective tissue that inextricably links you and the environment.

A Content Primer
What Is Water?

As the connective tissue of the environment, water is the principal transporter for all the essential nutrients, and the water cycle is the only one that connects all the interfaces of the Earth and its atmosphere (air-water and land-water, or vice versa). Water is a simple molecule composed of two hydrogen atoms and one oxygen atom (Figure 3.1), which are held together by strong bonds. Yet it is the simplicity of the molecule that gives it great versatility and importance.

FIGURE 3.1
Water Molecule

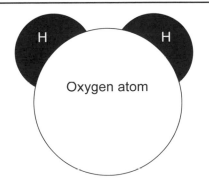

H   H

Oxygen atom

Water

Rain forest

Desert

Known as the *universal solvent,* water has the ability to carry dissolved elements, compounds, molecules, and nutrients from one place to another across the entire planet. In addition, water is a limiting factor in the function of essential nutrient cycles (see Chapter 5, Energy and Nutrients). For example, the decomposition of plant material in a tropical rain forest is exceptionally rapid when compared with the same process in a desert, even though these biomes have similar temperatures, because the rain forest is significantly wetter. This process results in the release and recycling of essential nutrients more quickly in a rainforest ecosystem as compared with a desert.

The Water Cycle

Precipitation is the manner in which water is returned to the Earth from the atmosphere. Once deposited on land water can take many pathways through an ecosystem. For example, water can

- be absorbed by soil and transferred to a plant through roots;

- travel through the ground and become part of the groundwater;

- run along the Earth's surface into a body of water, such as a stream, picking up minute amounts of dissolved salts and eventually making its way to the ocean; and

- be deposited on a mountaintop as snow or ice and remain locked or trapped there for many years.

Snow-covered mountain

The other main components of the water cycle include evaporation, condensation, evapotranspiration, and sublimation (see Figure 3.2). Visualizing the cyclical flow of water in this way provides a mental picture of the numerous possible pathways traversed by water in our ecosystem.

FIGURE 3.2
The Water Cycle

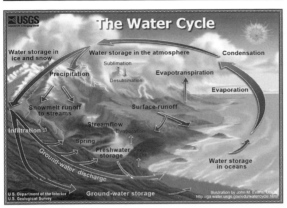

Source: U.S. Geological Survey, *http://ga.water.usgs.gov/edu/watercycle.html*

Other Aspects of Water

The pH, salinity, oxygen, and turbidity of water can greatly affect water's quality. Thus, we feel that the following content is essential for a fundamental understanding of the factors that impact the characteristics and quality of water.

pH in Water

As a measure of acidity, pH is dependent on the relative concentrations of hydrogen ions (H^+) in a solution. The scale of pH measurement (Figure 3.3) is 0–14. Solutions that measure 0–6 have a higher hydrogen ion concentration and are acidic; those that measure 8–14 have a lower hydrogen ion concentration and are alkaline (basic); and those that measure 7 are considered neutral.

The vast majority of aquatic organisms, particularly macroinvertebrates, are only able to tolerate fluctuations of pH levels within a narrow range of unit variation outside their preferred optimal range. Even small fluctuations in the pH of a body of water can have very serious consequences for the affected organisms (e.g., a pH change from 6.5 to 5.5).

Topic: pH Scale
Go to: *www.scilinks.org*
Code: IO014

Macroinvertebrate

There are several ways to measure pH; the most common methods use pH paper, a chemical test kit, or a pH meter. pH paper usually is packaged as small strips that students dip into the solution being tested; when they observe a color change, they compare it with a key in which different colors represent the values of the pH scale. Chemical kits involve the addition of an *indicator* solution to a sample of water and comparing the color change with a key in which different colors represent the values of the pH scale. A pH meter is a sort of electronic probe that directly measures pH (the hydrogen ion concentration) from the solution.

FIGURE 3.3
pH Scale

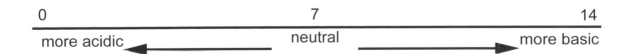

Salinity in Water

In our locale we are able to study freshwater at a local site and then move downstream into the larger watershed of the Chesapeake Bay, the nation's largest estuary (see Figure 3.4). By moving to the estuary we can add salinity as an additional water quality measurement.

FIGURE 3.4
Chesapeake Bay Map

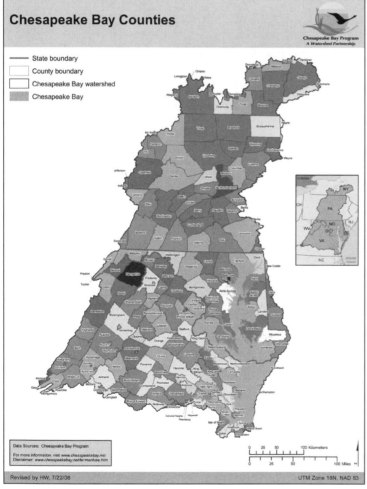

Source: Chesapeake Bay Program

What Is Salinity?

Nearly all water contains dissolved chemicals, even rainwater. We call these dissolved chemicals *salts*. The major dissolved salts (by element) found in seawater are 55.3% chlorine, 30.8% sodium, 3.7% magnesium, 2.6% sulfur, 1.2% calcium, and 1.1% potassium (Windows to the Universe 2002). Salinity is a measure of these dissolved salts in water and is calculated as the amount of salt (in grams) dissolved in 1,000 grams (or 1 liter) of seawater. Salinity, therefore, is represented as parts per thousand (ppt), meaning the number of grams of salt in 1 liter of seawater. For example, the salinity of normal ocean water is about 35 ppt (the range of salinity for ocean water is 32–37 ppt). This means that for every liter of seawater there are 35 grams of salt. In contrast, the salinity of brackish estuarine water is typically 0.5–17 ppt, and that of freshwater is less than 0.5 ppt.

What Causes Salinity?

Salts end up in aquatic ecosystems through relatively simple processes:

1. Rainwater falling on the land weathers and erodes rocks and rock fragments.

2. Rivers carry larger rock fragments as bed load, as they roll along the bottom of the stream. Smaller rock fragments and mineral grains are transported as suspended load (within the water column). Also included are ions or dissolved salts from the chemical weathering of rocks.

3. The weathering of other minerals and rocks also provides salts to the sea. For example, the calcite in limestone dissolves in slightly acidic natural waters, yielding calcium (Ca) and carbonate (CO_3).

FIGURE 3.5
Layering Salinity

separation or layering

Less dense freshwater from rivers and streams

More dense saltwater from the ocean or estuary

4. Streams and rivers then carry dissolved salts to the seas (an estimated 4 billion tons per year). Some of these dissolved solids will be deposited as sediment, so yearly gains may roughly balance sediment deposition. Salts have become concentrated in the sea from these many small deposits (compared with fresh water) and the Sun's heat causes the evaporation of water, leaving the salts behind. The most abundant mineral in seawater is sodium chloride (NaCl), or common sea salt.

Mountain spring

Modeling Salinity

Figures 3.5 and 3.6 illustrate how salinity affects the physical properties of water. Figure 3.5 illustrates the limited mixing between the less dense freshwater and the denser salt water of an estuary. In shallow estuaries the influx of ocean water creates a *salt wedge*, where the denser salt water, by tidal action, infiltrates under the less dense freshwater and creates a density gradient

FIGURE 3.6
Salt Wedge

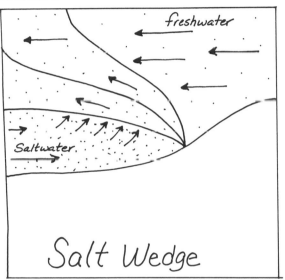

Source: Peter Cook, *http://omp.gso.uri.edu/ompweb/doee/img/imgindx1.htm*

SCILINKS
THE WORLD'S A CLICK AWAY

Topic: Solvation of Solids in Water

Go to: *www.scilinks.org*

Code: IO015

Topic: Freshwater Ecosystems

Go to: *www.scilinks.org*

Code: IO016

from the surface to the bottom (Figure 3.6). In this situation, the amount of freshwater and salt water varies by depth and impacts the types of organisms found.

Depending on a variety of factors, the estuary may be partially or fully mixed (Figures 3.7 and 3.8, p. 50). For example, in relatively shallow (20 feet) water with strong winds you may have complete mixing from the top to the bottom of the water column.

Measuring Salinity

It is important to measure salinity because, as with pH, certain organisms are naturally adapted for a

FIGURE 3.7
Partially Mixed Estuary

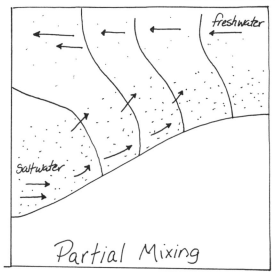

Source: Peter Cook, *http://omp.gso.uri.edu/ompweb/doee/img/imgindx1.htm*

FIGURE 3.8
Fully Mixed Estuary

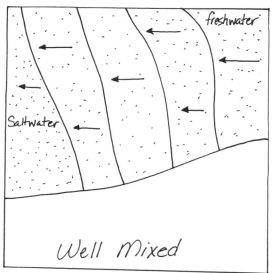

Source: Peter Cook, *http://omp.gso.uri.edu/ompweb/doee/img/imgindx1.htm*

specific range of salt tolerance within their environment. Salinity measurements play an important role in understanding water quality and have an impact on the diversity of life in an aquatic ecosystem. By measuring salinity some basic ideas about biodiversity can be predicted and can have an impact on species being studied, whether they are plant, animal, or microbe. For example, in a drought year with very little rainfall (freshwater) an estuary may become more salty (saline), leading to an increase in the appearance of organisms such as jellyfish and salt-tolerant fish. Thus, salinity will not only affect

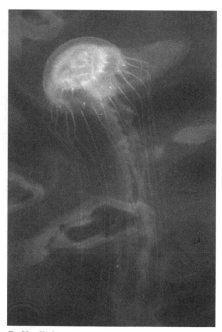

Jellyfish

the types of organisms present but also influence the biodiversity of the habitat.

In the early days of ship travel salinity was measured by collecting approximately 1 liter of seawater and allowing it to evaporate, leaving the salts behind. These salts were weighed and used to estimate salinity (thus the parts per thousand). Today salinity can be measured with a number of simple devices, including hydrometers.

Understanding a hydrometer reading requires a general understanding of what the reading indicates. The hydrometer measures the *specific gravity* of a liquid, which is the density of a substance divided by the density of water. For our purposes, the measurement indicates the density of the sample solution. Pure water has a specific gravity of 1 g/cm^3 and is used as our benchmark; ocean water has a specific gravity of about 33–37 g/cm^3. Any sample solution will be compared with the freshwater baseline, and, thus, any water that contains dissolved salts will show an increased density by having a measurement greater than 1 g/cm³ (Figure 3.9).

A hydrometer is basically a "bobber" in water. Students can construct their own hydrometer or buy a specific gravity instrument in a local aquarium shop. We have used one similar to the Aquarium Systems Instant Ocean Hydrometer. Instructions on making hydrometers can be found at the following websites:

* *www.csd509j.net/cvhs/berand/Marine/Labs/ Making%20Test%20Tube%20Hydrometers %20Student%20Guide.doc*

* *www.ecawa.asn.au/home/jfuller/liquids/ hydrometers.htm*

Oxygen in Water

Oxygen accounts for approximately 21% of the gas content of our atmosphere, with the majority consisting of nitrogen gas. We can think of the 21% as parts per hundred (pph), meaning that out of 100 molecules in a sample 21 of them would be oxygen. In lakes, ponds, streams, and oceans, however, *dissolved oxygen* (DO) is measured in parts per million (ppm); generally the range is 5–8 ppm. To convert from pph to ppm we multiply by 10,000 (the difference between 0.01, parts per hundred, and 0.000001, parts per million). Thus we find that the 21% of atmospheric oxygen is about 210,000 ppm, which is an enormous

disparity in concentration compared with the value of 8–9 ppm of DO in a pristine freshwater environment with a temperature range of 20–25°C. Understanding this difference (Table 3.1) between oxygen in air and oxygen in water makes us appreciate the adaptability of aquatic creatures, which allows them to survive on scarce amounts of oxygen—something that terrestrial organisms cannot do.

How Does Oxygen Get Into Water?

Oxygen gets into water from the atmosphere through the process of diffusion, moving from a place of higher concentration (in the air) to one of lower concentration (in the water). Other things that can help oxygen become dissolved in water include waves or wind, which disturbs the surface and allows for easier diffusion. Living aquatic organisms—namely, plants and algae—produce oxygen through photosynthesis and also add a considerable amount of DO to the aquatic system.

**FIGURE 3.9
A Hydrometer in a
Sample of Water
With Salt Added**

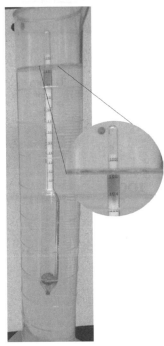

TABLE 3.1. Oxygen Values in Air Versus Water

	Oxygen in Air	Oxygen in Water*
Common values described	Constant, approximately 21% of air	Ranges from about 0 to 12 parts per million (ppm)
Comparison of parts per million values	210,000 ppm	0–12 ppm

* There are slight variations between freshwater and salt water—freshwater has a higher DO value at the same temperature as salt water because salt water has dissolved solids that take up space.

Temperature can also have an immense impact on DO levels. As the temperature of water rises, the gases that are dissolved in the water escape more easily because of increased molecular movement; as the temperature of water decreases, gases dissolved in the water are able to remain longer because there is less movement of the water molecules. Therefore, a general statement can be made that warmer water "holds" less oxygen than colder water.

Atmospheric pressure also has an impact on the DO concentration of water. In high pressure (at sea level or relatively close to sea level) oxygen can stay in the water more easily. An increase in elevation results in a decrease in pressure or the amount of "weight" on the water, allowing more gas to escape by diffusion.

FIGURE 3.10
Relationship of Dissolved Salts to Dissolved Oxygen

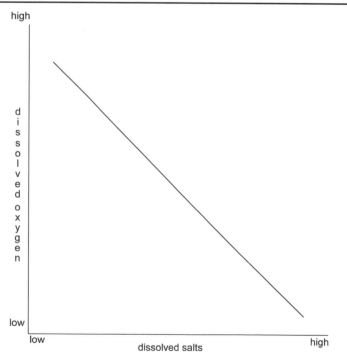

Finally, the amount of dissolved solids in water has an impact on DO concentrations. As the salinity increases, these dissolved solids take up more space and leave less space for the dissolved gases such as oxygen (Figure 3.10). Living in salt water therefore requires an organism to be highly adaptable to low DO levels, whereas living in freshwater, where there are fewer dissolved solids, does not require this degree of adaptability.

Measuring Dissolved Oxygen in Water

Because of the influences that temperature and pressure have on the amount of DO in water, getting an accurate DO reading can be difficult. Sophisticated measuring devices can compensate for both of these factors, but for many of us the cost is prohibitive.

When measuring the DO of a water sample, you must take the temperature into consideration and record it when the water is tested. (Remember that DO fluctuates with changing temperature.) Once these two values are recorded you can estimate the percent saturation of oxygen in water. It may be easier for students to understand percent saturation using the analogy of a sponge being full or partially full of water instead of referring to parts per million. Percent saturation is, thus, another means to represent the amount of available oxygen in water. With a percent saturation chart (Figure 3.11) students can estimate the percent saturation using the determined DO value and recorded temperature. The procedure is as follows:

1. Collect the water sample and immediately record the temperature.

2. Use a DO test kit (available from CHEMetrics, *www.chemetrics.com*) and determine the ppm value of that sample.

FIGURE 3.11
Percent Saturation of Oxygen

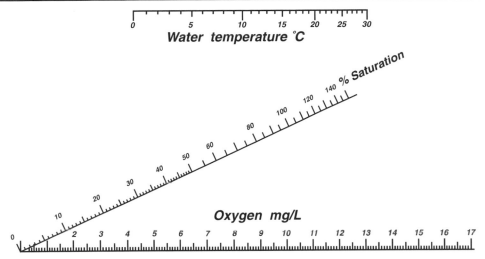

Source: Water on the Web, *http://wateronthewer.org/under/waterquality/oxygen.html*

3. Use a straightedge to connect a line on the diagram between the two points (°C and ppm). For example, a 23°C sample of water with a DO value of 5 mg/L (ppm) has about 62% oxygen saturated in solution.

The University of Wisconsin Extension website has more resources on DO and percent saturation: *http://watermonitoring.uwex.edu/wav/monitoring/oxygen.html*. When performing DO tests, use indirectly vented chemical splash goggles and gloves. Maker sure there is appropriate ventilation. Review MSDS prior to using DO kit chemicals. Washi hands with soap and water after completing tests.

Soil in Water
Transparency and Turbidity

Simply defined, *turbidity* is the relative measure of the transparency (or cloudiness) of a body of water due to an increase in suspended substances in the water column. Suspended substances can be abiotic in origin (e.g., soil) or biotic (e.g., zooplankton and phytoplankton).

The "cloudiness" determines the depth at which light can penetrate. *Transparency* is a term that describes how far light can penetrate into a water column before it completely dissipates. The reason turbidity and transparency are important for understanding the biotic nature of the aquatic habitat is because the depth of light penetration is directly linked to important features of the aquatic environment, such as supporting the growth of submerged aquatic vegetation. Our goal here is to focus on the basic concept of transparency as it is related to the cloudiness of water (see also *http://watermonitoring.uwex.edu/wav/monitoring/transparency.html*).

Measuring Transparency

You can use a Secchi disk to measure transparency of slow-moving, deep bodies of water such as ponds, lakes, or bays. A Secchi disk is a black-and-white plate, 20 cm in diameter, that is lowered into the water column (see Figures 3.12 and 3.13, p. 54).

FIGURE 3.12
Secchi Disk

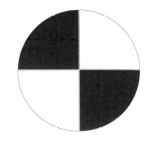

FIGURE 3.13
Using a Secchi Disk to Measure Transparency

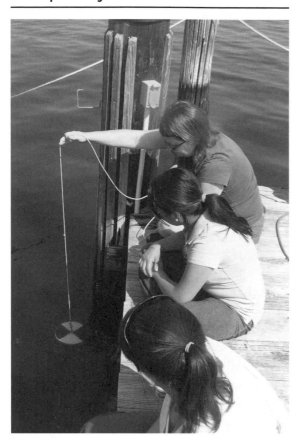

FIGURE 3.14
Turbidity Tube With Water Sample

FIGURE 3.15
Turbidity Tube Showing Visible Secchi Disk at Bottom of Tube

The depth in meters at which the dish just disappears is called the Secchi depth and is a relative measure of the water's transparency.

For stream measurements, you can use a *turbidity tube*, which consists of a long plastic tube containing a small Secchi disk at its bottom. Water is added to the tube, which acts as the water column, and the transparency is determined by the height of the water in the tube when the Secchi disk is no longer visible (see Figures 3.14 and 3.15). This measurement gives a relative value of transparency of the water, with a greater value signifying higher transparency and a lower value signifying lower transparency.

Water Activities

You will notice that a number of these activities are initially conducted inside the classroom. Our reasoning is to have the students practice the procedures before using them in the field and to allow students to gain a better understanding of the fundamental content and concepts involved.

Activity 1. Modeling the Water Cycle

This activity uses basic materials to demonstrate condensation and precipitation of the water cycle as well as phase changes of water. The setup is simple yet can lead to other inquiry activities.

Driving Question

What stages of the water cycle are demonstrated by water of different temperatures?

Materials

- Three containers, each half-full of water (good containers are clear plastic 2-liter bottles or clear plastic storage containers or jars with a screw cap lid; see Figure 3.16):

  1. One has room temperature water (approx. 20°C).

  2. One has hot water from the tap (approx. 40°C). (Use caution when working with hot water from the tap, as it can cause skin burns.)

  3. One has cold water (add a few ice cubes and let them melt, approx. 10°C).

- Indirectly vented chemical splash goggles

Procedure

1. Divide the class into groups of no more than three and ask the group to write down

FIGURE 3.16
Water Cycle Model

Water Cycle Data Sheet

Water Temperature	Cold (with some ice cubes melted)	Room Temperature	Hot (hot water from the tap)
Observation after 5 minutes			
Observation after 10 minutes			
Observation after 20 minutes			

observations about changes in the three containers over time on their data sheet.

2. To help them make connections to what they see, ask groups to make illustrations.

3. Have each group share their observations with another group and develop some conclusions about how the containers are different (e.g., one jar has hot water, one jar has condensation on the outside).

Think About

1. Share observations and illustrations with the whole class and develop some consensus about the containers, their contents, and how the observations relate to the phases of the water cycle.

2. Predict what you would observe if we left these water containers on the table over the weekend.

3. How would your predictions change if we left the water containers outside over the weekend?

4. Think about your car windows in the winter, or the mirror in the bathroom after you take a shower. Think about how you can draw pictures on the window or the mirror. Describe what parts of the water cycle this demonstrates.

Activity 2. Preparing pH Indicators From Red Cabbage

Red cabbage juice (RCJ) makes an excellent pH indicator, is easy to prepare, and is a fun introduction for students to the concepts of acids, bases, and pH. There are a couple of standard ways to extract RCJ and the key pigment anthocyanin.

Driving Question

How can cabbage juice be turned into a tool to measure pH?

The Boiling Method Materials

- One small head of red cabbage

- Small pot half-filled with distilled water (available at grocery stores)

- Heat source (if electrical hot plate, use a GFI-protected circuit)

- A 500 ml beaker or flask (available from any science education supplier [e.g., Science Kit & Boreal Laboratories, *http://sciencekit.com/ Default.asp?bhcd2=1257261644*])

- Indirectly vented chemical splash goggles, heat gloves, and aprons

Procedure

1. Chop up the red cabbage and place it in a pan with enough distilled water to cover it.

2. Boil until the water turns a dark red-purple color. Use caution, as the splashing of hot liquid can burn skin.

3. Pour off the liquid once it cools. Strain using cheesecloth if needed to remove large particles.

The "Juicer" Method **Materials**

• One small head of red cabbage

• Small pot half-filled with distilled water

• Juicer (obtained in kitchen supply section of department store)

• A 500 ml beaker or flask

• Indirectly vented chemical splash goggles

Procedure

1. Chop up the red cabbage and run it through a juicer.

2. Take the extracted juice and dilute it with distilled water (2 parts juice to 1 part water) so that it thins out a bit and is more translucent. Strain using cheesecloth if needed to remove large particles.

Activity 3. Red Cabbage Juice as a pH Indicator: Developing pH Standards

Once the RCJ solution is prepared, it can be added to a variety of household products to "indicate" what the pH may be. Changes in the color of the RCJ are due to the behavior of the pigment anthocyanin at different pH levels. For example, pink-orange colors indicate acidic solutions, blue colors (royal blue to purple) indicate neutral pH, and blue-green colors indicate alkaline (basic). This activity will use three household solutions (vinegar, water, and baking soda) to prepare the standards used for testing in Activity 4.

Driving Questions

1. How will different household solutions (vinegar, water, and baking soda) react with a homemade pH indicator?

2. How will the pH of different household solutions (vinegar, water, and baking soda) compare with each other?

Materials

• Prepared RCJ extract

• Three small, clear containers (test tubes [available from any science education supplier] or baby food jars)

• Eyedropper (available from any science education supplier)

• Standard test solutions (vinegar, water, and baking soda)

• Indirectly vented chemical splash goggles and aprons

Procedure

1. Add two teaspoons of vinegar, water, and baking soda solution to each of the three small containers (test tubes or baby food jars).

Standard Indicators for Red Cabbage Juice

	Acid	Neutral	Base
	Vinegar	Water	Baking soda
Color of RCJ with test sample	Pink-orange	Blue (royal to purple)	Blue-green

5. Which household products are acidic? Basic? Neutral? Explain your reasoning.

6. Which product contains the highest concentration of hydrogen ions? Which contains the lowest? Explain your reasoning.

7. Many commercial products are advertised as pH balanced. Explain what is meant by the term *pH balanced*.

8. Describe the observations and measurements you made about the three water samples from the environment. How did these samples compare with the household products that were tested?

Activity 5. Modeling the Impact of Salinity in Water

This activity is a simple exploratory demonstration about salinity using an egg and a beaker of water.

Driving Question

How will an egg placed in water behave differently when salt is added to water?

Materials

- Egg (raw or hard-boiled)
- Clear container
- Tablespoon
- Stirring rod (available from any science education supplier)
- Table salt
- Indirectly vented chemical splash goggles and aprons

Procedure

1. Fill container three-quarters full with water.

FIGURE 3.18
Eggs in Water

2. Have students predict what the egg will do when placed in water (see Figure 3.18).

3. Add salt to the water (one heaping tablespoon at a time) and ask them to predict what will happen to the egg.

Think About

1. Explain why the egg behaved the way it did in freshwater.

2. Explain why the egg behaved the way it did when salt was added to the freshwater.

3. Describe the differences between water without salt and water with salt.

4. The Dead Sea is one of the world's saltiest bodies of water, with a salinity of 33.7%. Think of a time you tried to float in your neighborhood pool. Compare this experience with what you think it would be like to try to float in the Dead Sea.

Activity 6. Exploring the Impact of Temperature and Salinity on Water Density

Another activity that provides a concrete example of salinity and water involves placing low- and high-salinity water into the same container. This activity will be conducted in three parts. For Part III refer to the "Modeling Salinity" section earlier in this chapter for a review of the properties of the interaction of freshwater and salt water.

Driving Question

How is the mixing of water affected by temperature and salinity?

Materials
(for each part)

- Clear containers (beakers, pasta storage containers, etc.)

- Hot (40°C) and cold (10°C) tap water

- Table salt (mixed as 1 liter of water with 35 g of salt)

- Measuring cups for pouring (8 oz)

- Blue and yellow food coloring (available in the baking aisle of the supermarket)

- Indirectly vented chemical splash goggles

Procedure
Part I. Room Temperature Samples

1. Pour water into one container so it is about one-third full. Add 5 drops of blue food coloring and mix thoroughly.

2. In separate container repeat the same procedure using yellow food coloring.

3. Tilt the blue container and slowly pour yellow water along the inside of the blue container so as not to splash or disturb blue water.

4. Describe and diagram the results.

5. Explain what happened and why.

Part II. Cold Versus Hot Water Samples

1. Color cold water blue. Repeat sequence of pouring as outlined in Part I.

2. Describe and diagram the results.

3. Explain what happened and why.

Part III. Salt and Non-Salt Samples

1. Use two room temperature samples.

2. Color the salt solution blue.

3. Color the non-salt solution yellow.

4. Repeat sequence of pouring as outlined in Part I.

5. Describe and diagram the results.

6. Explain what happened and why.

Think About

1. What happened when the cold water and hot water samples were combined? Using your understanding of density, explain why this happened.

2. What happened when the salt solution and non-salt solution samples were combined? Using your understanding of density, explain why this happened.

Expected Results

- Room temperature samples mix completely and water turns green.

- Careful pouring will improve separation of cold and hot water samples, with cold (blue) staying at the bottom because of greater density than hot (yellow).

- Salt and non-salt samples separate, with salt staying at the bottom because of greater

FIGURE 3.19
Layered Solution of Samples With Differing Salinities

density than non-salt. In Figure 3.19 layers of water with varying salinities are displayed (higher salinity on the bottom).

Ideal results illustrate the impact that temperature and salinity have on the density of water and its ability to mix or not mix (form layers).

Activity 7. Sponging Up the Dissolved Oxygen

This activity models the concept of percent saturation using simple materials and practice. Teachers and students can use the percent saturation chart to gain a better understanding of the relationship among percent saturation, DO

FIGURE 3.20
Use of Sponge to Demonstrate Percent Saturation

Sponges can be used to investigate the concept of percent saturation and dissolved oxygen and provide a good method for practicing estimation and math concepts.

measurements, and temperature. For the purpose of this activity the sponge (Figure 3.20) equates to the aquatic ecosystem and the water represents the DO.

Driving Questions

1. How do fish and aquatic organisms get the oxygen they need to breathe?

2. How can you determine the amount of oxygen in water?

Materials
(per team)

- One small kitchen sponge

- One 250–500 ml graduated cylinder (available from any science education supplier)

- One shallow pan

- One 16 oz cup

- Stick thermometer in °C (available from Science Kit & Boreal Laboratories, *http://sciencekit.com/Default.asp?bhcd2=1257261644*)

- Water

- Percent saturation chart (Figure 3.11, p. 53)

- Safety glasses or goggles and aprons

Procedure
Part I. Determining 100% Saturation

1. Add water to the shallow pan so it is about half-full and let the sponge soak until completely saturated.

2. Remove the sponge and carefully squeeze as much water as possible from the sponge into the cup.

3. Pour water from the cup into the graduated cylinder and record the volume. This is the 100% saturation value.

4. Pour water from the graduated cylinder back into the pan so it is ready for the next measurement.

Part II. Target Saturation Levels

The goal of Part II is to attain a better understanding of percent saturation and not necessarily to attain a perfect result (i.e., getting the exact target value). Students should attempt to attain saturation levels of 50% and 25%.

1. Place the sponge in the shallow pan until approximately 50% saturated. (This may happen quickly. Encourage students to experiment with different methods of getting 50% saturation.)

2. Remove the sponge and carefully squeeze water from the sponge into the cup.

3. Pour water from the cup into the graduated cylinder and record the volume.

4. Using the volume from Part I as 100% saturation, calculate the percent saturation of this sample. Repeat the procedure and attempt to attain a 50% saturation level. Sample calculation:

$$Percent\ Saturation - \frac{volume\ of\ water\ from\ Part\ II}{volume\ of\ water\ from\ Part\ I} \times 100$$

5. Repeat the procedure and attempt to attain a 25% saturation level.

Part III. Estimating the Amount (in ppm) of Dissolved Oxygen

Once Part II is completed use the percent saturation chart (Figure 3.11, p. 53) to estimate the amount of DO (ppm) at each value of percent saturation for the given temperature. Record these amounts on the data sheet.

Think About

1. Why would we use a sponge to help us model percent saturation?

2. Describe the differences between your measurements for volume in 25% saturation and 50% saturation.

3. How do the results described in question 2 compare with the differences you see between your measurements for volume in 50% and 100% saturation?

Topic: Solubility
Go to: *www.scilinks.org*
Code: IO017

Activity 8. Testing Solubility of Oxygen in Water Over Time

Dissolved oxygen can be the basis of simple exploration activities that incorporate testing samples over time. This is an open-ended activity related to understanding the influence of factors on DO. The basic idea is to collect a sample of water, immediately test it using a DO test kit, and then explore different factors that will affect the ability of the oxygen to remain dissolved.

Percent (%) Saturation and Estimated ppm of Dissolved Oxygen (DO) Data Sheet

% Saturation Target Value	Volume (ml)	Temperature (°C)	Estimated ppm DO
100			
50			
25			

Driving Questions

1. How does the temperature of water affect the percent DO in a water sample?

2. How does the percent DO change in a water sample over time?

Materials

- DO test kit (available from CHEMetrics [*www.chemetrics.com*] and LaMotte Company [*www.lamotte.com*]—the latter has the Earth Force Elementary Education Watershed Field Trip kit and the Pondwater Tour kit)

- A 2-liter sample of tap water or aquarium water

- Indirectly vented chemical splash goggles, gloves, and aprons

FIGURE 3.21
Changes in Dissolved Oxygen Over Time

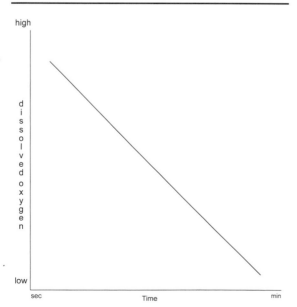

- Stick thermometer (available from Science Kit & Boreal Laboratories, *http://sciencekit.com/Default.asp?bhcd2=1257261644*)

- Indirectly vented chemical splash goggles, gloves, and aprons

Procedure

1. Use appropriate ventilation. Obtain a sample of water.

2. Test DO immediately, and measure the temperature.

3. Set the sample aside and repeat the test at 15-minute intervals (see Figure 3.21).

Think About

1. What patterns did you notice in measure of percent DO over time?

2. How do you think the results would be different if we started with boiling water and monitored changes over time?

3. How do you think the results would be different if we started with ice water and monitored changes over time?

4. How do you think the results would be different if we started with salt water and monitored changes over time?

This activity can be extended by incorporating different variables, such as a change in temperature (heating or cooling), agitation by manual stirring or other means, exposure to light and dark, and any other factors proposed by the students. The fundamental concept for students to understand is that DO levels fluctuate in water and that this change can be influenced by any number of factors (temperature, salinity, agitation).

Activity 9. Modeling Turbidity

This activity can be used to help students understand how to (1) model the cause of turbidity in water and (2) identify soil composition by sedimentation (see Chapter 4, Soil: It's Not Dirt).

Driving Question

What materials can be found in water, and how can you separate them?

Materials

- Clear jar with lid (Mason jars or canning jars work well)
- Tap water
- Soil sample
- Safety glasses or goggles, aprons, gloves

Procedure

1. Fill approximately one-third of the jar with soil.
2. Fill jar with water, leaving 1 inch of space at top.
3. Put lid on and shake vigorously for five minutes.
4. Stop shaking and observe the particles in the soil (see Figure 3.22).
5. Once observations are complete, set the jar aside for use in Chapter 4 and the activity on soil composition. Wash hands with soap and water.

Think About

1. Describe your observations of the water immediately after shaking.
   a. Have you ever seen water like this in a river or stream? What caused it to look like this?

FIGURE 3.22
Two Soil Samples

Two sediment samples illustrating components of soil texture: On the left is a sample from a mountain spring, and on the right is a sample from a river.

   b. Describe at least one way water in this condition could affect aquatic life.

2. Describe your observations of the water after the particles have settled. Do you notice anything unique about how the particles have settled?

Have students compare and contrast the particles that settle to the bottom first and those that remain suspended. Challenge them to use their observations to discuss the following question: Do you think that the differences in the sizes of these particles affect which ones take longer to settle? (See Figure 3.23 as an example.)

FIGURE 3.23
Sedimentator

Activity 10. Measuring Turbidity With a Turbidity Tube

Initial use of the turbidity tube can be conducted in the classroom using prepared samples. The purpose of this activity is to have students practice using the tube so they become efficient when using one in the field.

Driving Question

How does the turbidity of water change as the amount of soil in the water increases?

Part I. Making a Turbidity Tube

For Part I of this activity we refer you to the GLOBE (**G**lobal **L**earning and **O**bservations to **B**enefit the **E**nvironment) Program and their instructions on making this tool (*http://cartt.4j. lane.edu/ve/globe/globedata/Turbidity.pdf*). See also Figure 3.14, earlier in this chapter (p. 54).

Part II. Preparing Water and Soil Samples Materials

- Four gallons of water

- Soil

- Indirectly vented chemical splash goggles, gloves, aprons (use also for Part III)

Procedure

1. Make four samples of water and soil. Begin with one gallon of water for each sample and add the following amounts of soil:

- Sample 1: ¼ cup of soil

- Sample 2: ½ cup of soil

- Sample 3: ¾ cup of soil

- Sample 4: 1 cup of soil

2. Shake vigorously and set aside for 15–20 minutes, until all large particles have settled out.

Part III. Measuring Turbidity Materials

- Turbidity tube

- Water and soil samples prepared in Part II

Procedure

1. Pour first water sample into the turbidity tube until the Secchi disk is no longer visible when viewing the contents of the tube from the opening in the top.

2. Record the depth of water to the nearest 1 cm on the data sheet.

3. Repeat steps 1 and 2 with the remaining water samples. Wash hands with soap and water.

Have students create a line graph (y axis = depth of water to see Secchi disk in centimeters, x axis = amount of soil [e.g., ¼ cup, ½ cup, ¾ cup, and 1 cup], p. 67) to organize their data on the four water samples. Encourage them to review the data and draw conclusions about the impact the soil content of a water sample has on its turbidity reading. Use the data sheet for comparing

Turbidity Reading Data Sheet

	¼ cup soil	½ cup soil	¾ soil	1 cup soil
Turbidity reading (depth reading in cm)				

differing amounts of soil and sediment and the effect of these differing amounts on a turbidity reading.

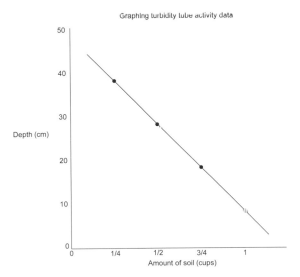

Turbidity tube graph

Think About

1. Review the data from the data sheet and the line graph you constructed to organize your turbidity data. What impact did the soil content of a water sample have on its turbidity reading?

2. Use your data and observations to predict what the turbidity reading might be in a mixture of 1 gallon of water and $\frac{1}{8}$ cup of soil. Explain your prediction.

3. Use your data and observations to predict what the turbidity reading might be in a mixture of 1 gallon of water and 2 cups of soil. Explain your prediction.

4. Looking at the samples in Figure 3.24, what can you conclude about the turbidity of this body of water?

FIGURE 3.24
Turbidity Tube Sequence From Monocacy River, Frederick, MD

Wrap-Up

Our goal in this chapter was to provide enough varied activities to help students gain a keener understanding of the role that water plays in the living world. While not an exhaustive list, these experiences will engage students in the purposeful study of the components that affect water and ways to go about measuring them. All of these activities have a direct application to field-based studies, and it is our hope that students will be encouraged to study the local aquatic ecosystems.

Resource List
Websites
CHEMetrics
   www.chemetrics.com
GLOBE (Global Learning and Observations to Benefit the Environment)
   http://cartt.4j.lane.edu/ve/globe/globedata/Turbidity.pdf

Water Activities

Hydrometers

*www.csd509j.net/cvhs/berand/Marine/
Labs/Making%20Test%20Tube%20
Hydrometers%20Student%20Guide.doc
www.ecawa.asn.au/home/jfuller/liquids/
hydrometers.htm*

LaMotte Company water quality testing products

www.lamotte.com

Red cabbage chemistry

*www.chemistryland.com/CHM107Lab/Lab1/
Lab1PreparingCabbageExtract.htm*

Ship Mates ("Ocean Salinity")

www.bigelow.org/shipmates/salinity.html

University of Wisconsin Extension

"Dissolved Oxygen": *http://watermonitoring.
uwex.edu/wav/monitoring/oxygen.html*
"Transparency": *http://watermonitoring.uwex.
edu/wav/monitoring/transparency.html*

Windows to the Universe, University
Corporation for Atmospheric Research

*www.windows.ucar.edu/tour/link=/earth/
Water/dissolved_salts.html&edu=high*

4

Soil: It's Not Dirt

Dirt, soil, what's the difference? Good question. Let's think about this before delving into our soil content primer. We'll start with simply gathering a sample of each one. Sweep the floor in your home and you'll have what most of us refer to as dirt, or just get a sample from the vacuum cleaner if you dare. What you'll discover is that dirt is composed of crumbs, hair, lint, skin cells, and the unfortunate arthropod (e.g., an ant). Okay, so what is soil? Dig up a sample of earth from your backyard or obtain some potting soil and you'll basically have three components: sand, silt, and clay. Not very exciting—but it can be with some basic information and investigative inquiry techniques.

A Content Primer

Learning about soil and soil composition is an essential part of environmental science education and connects the land-water and land-air interface in a number of significant ways. For example, soil structure and chemical composition are clear indicators of the usefulness of soil to grow plants, which is important for a healthy ecosystem. By learning about important aspects of soil and its significance in the environment, a better understanding of watersheds, nutrient cycles, water quality, and overall quality of the system can be attained.

Soil: It's Not Dirt

What Is Soil?

By definition soil is composed of both *abiotic* components, such as sand, silt, and clay from the weathering and erosion of geological sources, and *biotic* material, organic matter from the decay of plants, animals, and other organisms. Soil is a thin layer atop the portion of the Earth known as the crust, which together with the uppermost mantle makes up the Earth's lithosphere (see Figure 4.1). This layer extends into the aquatic and marine environment (typically termed *sediment*) as well and can vary widely in its thickness and composition.

FIGURE 4.1
Earth Cross-Section

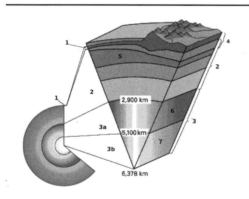

Key
1 = crust (oceanic and continental crust 0–80 km)
2 = mantle (upper mantle, including asthenosphere, and lower mantle)
3 = core (3a = outer core, 3b = inner core)
4 = lithosphere (crust and uppermost solid mantle)
5 = asthenosphere
6 = outer core liquid
7 = inner core solid
Source: *http://pubs.usgs.gov/gip/dynamic/inside.html*

Soil can be divided into *soil horizons*, defined as "relatively uniform *soil* layer[s] which lies at any depth in the soil profile, which is parallel, or nearly so, with the soil surface, and which is differentiated from adjacent horizons above and below by contrasts in mineral or organic properties"

(Allaby and Allaby 1999). Soil horizons can then be categorized by the layer's composition. The typical horizon layers are O, A, E, B, C, and R; the R horizon is the underlying bedrock (see Figure 4.2). There can be significant variations in soil composition, and the composition is helpful to

FIGURE 4.2
Soil Cross-Section Illustrating Some of the Horizons Found in Soil

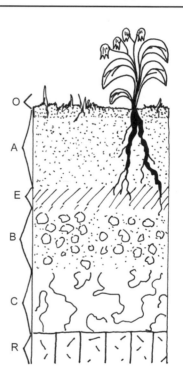

O is the top layer of soil and contains high levels of organic material (litter). A is the start of mineral soil components and mixes with organic materials. E is the layer where leaching is dominant and removes organic material, inorganic material, and clay from the soil; this process is driven by the movement of water through the soil. B is the layer where minerals and fine sediments start to become compacted. C is the layer where the soil parent material is found. R is the layer of bedrock.

indicate the environment of origin (e.g., loamy temperate forest soil compared with sandy soil from the coastal plain).

Soil Morphology
Color

All soils can be classified using three basic categories: *color*, *structure*, and *texture* (Lal 2002). One of the first things you will observe about soil is the color. Soil color is influenced by sedimentation from sources that carry minerals, primarily iron as well as organic matter (Lal 2002). Iron in soil creates a reddish-orange color in dry material and becomes increasingly more yellow as the moisture increases. Decomposed organic matter (dead plants and animals), known as *humus*, is black. The variety of sources will result in color variations that can be interpreted with practice and knowledge of the surrounding environment (see Table 4.1).

Another influence on soil color is the amount of aeration or oxygen available in soil, which then dictates biological activity. Oxygen makes

TABLE 4.1
Sources of Soil Color

Soil Color	Source of Color
Reddish-orange	Presence of iron oxides
Black	Presence of organic matter, manganese oxides, or iron sulfides. Organic matter can indicate that the soil is nutrient rich and fertile. Iron sulfides occur in wetlands and are often associated with the rotten egg odor found in wetlands; this odor is produced via sulfide gas from iron sulfide formation.
Gray	Presence of elevated water tables and reduced iron.

Topic: Soil Types
Go to: *www.scilinks.org*
Code: IO022

TABLE 4.2
Influences of Soil Condition on Color

Condition	Dark (dark grayish-black)	Moderately Dark (brown to yellow brown)	Light (pale brown, yellow)
Organic matter	High	Medium	Low
Erosion factor	Low	Medium	High
Aeration	High	Medium	Low
Available nitrogen	High	Medium	Low
Fertility	High	Medium	Low
Soil Condition	**Subsurface Soil Color**		
Water-logged soils, poor aeration	Grayish-black (if in low-rainfall soils 0–20 inches)		
Well-drained soils	Yellow, red-brown, black (if in forest soils)		
Somewhat poorly drained soils	Mottled gray (if in humid soils)		

Source: Adapted from BioWorld Products, *www.adbio.com/science/soil/color.htm*

soil either *aerobic* (oxygen rich) or *anaerobic* (oxygen poor). Moisture also plays a role in soil conditions (the amount of rainfall; the proximity to a stream or a source of groundwater such as a natural spring) and further impacts the striking variations in color of similar soil samples under different conditions (see Table 4.2, p. 71).

Structure

Soil structure is simply the organization of soil clumps, or aggregates, into an arrangement that determines how well water will drain through the soil. For example, soil in a temperate forest generally has a spongy consistency, composed of organic matter that disaggregates easily (falls apart) and is porous, which provides filtration and good drainage. The photo in Figure 4.3 shows the soil from a forest floor and the overall structure, including bits of leaves, woody materials, and decomposed organic matter.

FIGURE 4.3
Soil From a Forest in Frederick County, MD, Illustrating the Overall Structure of the Uppermost Soil Horizon

Drainage is one factor that makes forest cover on land so valuable to water quality because instead of water runoff, the soil acts to filter, or "percolate," water, thus replenishing

groundwater sources and helping the water remain clear. In contrast, highly compacted soil or impervious surfaces (think of a parking lot) will result in poor percolation and more runoff, leading to more sedimentation and contaminants in streams and other water bodies.

Texture

There are 12 soil texture classes identified in the *Soil Survey Manual* of the U.S. Department of Agriculture (USDA) Natural Resources Conservation Service (see Figure 4.4). These classes are primarily determined by biotic material and

FIGURE 4.4
Soil Texture Triangle for Soil Composition Determination

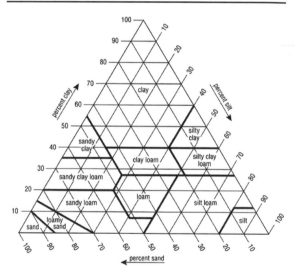

Source: U.S. Department of Agriculture, Natural Resources Conservation Service. 2007. *Soil survey manual*, Chapter 3: Examination and description of soils. *http://soils.usda.gov/technical/manual/contents/chapter3e.html*

by three primary abiotic components: sand, silt, and clay. The smaller-sized particles are called *fine earth* and are distinct from *rock fragments* (pebbles, cobbles, stones, and boulders) by size (USDA 2007). Fine earth particles are generally

TABLE 4.3
Fine Earth Particle Size Comparison

Name	Size (mm)
Very coarse sand	2.0–1.0
Coarse sand	1.0–0.5
Medium sand	0.5–0.25
Fine sand	0.25–0.10
Very fine sand	0.10–0.05
Silt	0.05–0.002
Clay	< 0.002

Source: U.S. Department of Agriculture, Natural Resources Conservation Service, *http://soils.usda.gov/technical/manual/contents/chapter3e.html#50*

less than 2 mm in diameter (see Table 4.3) and are determined in the field by feel. Although classifying soil type can be somewhat complicated, the texture triangle in Figure 4.4 makes this process easier, yet goes beyond simply calling a soil sample clay, silt, or sand.

What does texture tell us? Soils that have a certain composition will have specific characteristics that determine their texture classification and in part their function. For example, a predominance of sand would create a soil with very little ability to retain moisture, whereas a predominance of clay would create a soil that is very "sticky" or compact when wet, providing very little, if any, drainage. Soils that are considered optimal for plant growth are known as loam or sandy loam and are medium-textured soils with relatively good drainage. A medium texture provides more pore space that allows for water percolation/filtration and gas exchange—crucial processes for soil-dwelling organisms. Soil components such as sand and silt are a result of physical weathering, and clay is a result of chemical weathering. Clay becomes significant in the land-water interface because it will carry nutrients and other minerals that become bound to its structure chemically to sources of water through erosion and runoff, thus contributing negatively to water clarity. Too much clay from runoff, as depicted in Figure 4.5, can result in too many nutrients in a system.

FIGURE 4.5
Monocacy River (MD) Runoff

Plume of sediment runoff in the Monocacy River

Soil as a Habitat

Although most of us may think of soil as consisting of only abiotic components, it is closely tied to a myriad of organisms (see, e.g., Figure 4.6) that make it their home. Think of the interactions and processes of organisms that alter the soil makeup. For example, digestive processing by earthworms and their addition of organic material (poop) to soil and the many varieties of bacteria that inhabit soil can change the soil's composition of nutrients (Discovery Education). Bacteria, in particular, are very closely integrated to soil types (and sediment in the aquatic environment) and are the subject of continuing research and study by scientists, leading to new findings about the importance of these microscopic soil inhabitants.

FIGURE 4.6
Centipede and Fungus

Soil: It's Not Dirt

It is helpful to understand soil basics when considering environmental science education and outdoor activities, because the type of soil can provide clues to the health of the surrounding habitat and an essential link to the land-water and land-air interfaces.

Soil Activities

Soil studies are easy for many teachers to ignore because unless a school site has construction going on, soil is typically covered with grass or pavement and therefore "invisible" to students. Because we don't see much soil, it is convenient to think of it as simple, uniform, and unimportant. Studying soil or "dirt," however, is an excellent inquiry project that integrates science process skills, mainly observing, classifying, comparing/contrasting, and inferring. A soil system plays an integral role in environmental studies because (1) most living organisms either live or make their living from a relationship with soil, and (2) soil is a vital component of nutrient cycles.

The activities that follow will investigate the general soil characteristics of color, structure, and texture and will link the soil environment to biology by showcasing a variety of soil-dwelling bacteria that can be seen with the naked eye through the construction of a Winogradsky column.

Activity 1. Soil Color: Wetland Versus Nonwetland Soils[1]

We begin with a soil color activity," Do You Dig Wetland Soil?" from *WOW! The Wonders of Wetlands* (Kesselheim et al. 1995), an activity book published by Environmental Concern. Although Environmental Concern focuses mainly on the study of wetlands, this is the simplest and most inexpensive (and therefore the best) activity we have found that engages students directly in handling soil as they investigate soil color.

Wetland soils, called *hydric*, can be identified by their grayish-black color; this color can be attributed to the prolonged saturation of these soils, resulting in little aerobic activity.

---

[1] "Do You Dig Wetland Soil?" activity (p. 76) from *WOW! The Wonders of Wetlands* is used with permission from Environmental Concern Inc. For further information contact Environmental Concern Inc. at PO Box P, 201 Boundary Lane, St. Michaels, MD 21663. Ph: 410-745-9620, or visit *www.wetland.org*.

Driving Questions

1. What are the characteristics of wetland soil?

2. How can we distinguish wetland soil from nonwetland soil?

Materials

- Soil color chart (Figure 4.7, p. 76; see the Wetland Soils Color Chart in the "Do You Dig Wetland Soils?" activity [Kesselheim et al. 1995] for the color representations)

- 64-count box of Crayola crayons

- Trowel, shovel, or soil corer (available at lawn and garden stores)

- Bucket or container for soil

- Meterstick or tape measure to measure depth of soil sample

- Safety glasses or goggles

Procedure

1. Create field identification charts using crayons.

2. Collect a soil sample and use the Wetland Soils Color Chart to make a general determination if soil is upland or wetland in origin.

3. Use the Wetland Soils Color Chart to make a specific color identification.

Think About

1. What soil characteristics did you observe?

2. How did soil from the bottom of the hole differ from soil near the surface in color and texture?

3. Compare wetland soil with soil you have observed at home and around the schoolyard. How do the soils differ, and what makes them different?

Topic: Soil and Climate
Go to: *www.scilinks.org*
Code: IO023

Topic: Wetlands
Go to: *www.scilinks.org*
Code: IO024

FIGURE 4.7
"Do You Dig Wetland Soil?" Identification Chart and Color Schemes From Wonders of Wetland Program

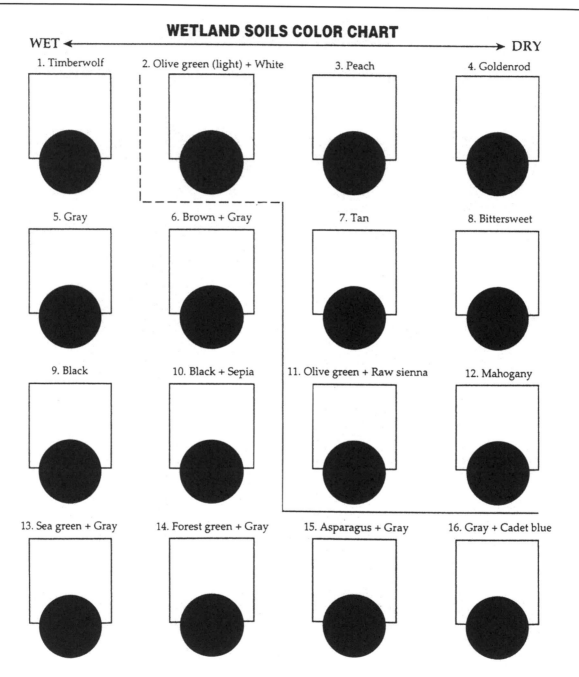

WETLAND SOILS COLOR CHART

WET ← → DRY

1. Timberwolf
2. Olive green (light) + White
3. Peach
4. Goldenrod

5. Gray
6. Brown + Gray
7. Tan
8. Bittersweet

9. Black
10. Black + Sepia
11. Olive green + Raw sienna
12. Mahogany

13. Sea green + Gray
14. Forest green + Gray
15. Asparagus + Gray
16. Gray + Cadet blue

Activity 2. Soil Texture Investigation

An important part of studying soil is learning what soil is composed of, how these components differ, and the compositional parts of a sample. If you recall in Chapter 3, Activity 9, we used a jar of soil and water (the sedimentator) to determine the relative turbidity of water. In this activity we return to the sedimentator and ask students to describe what they see. To refresh their memories, it may be useful to prepare another sample so they can view the remixing of the particles (Figure 4.8). During the initial mixing phase (immediately after shaking) students can make observations of the settling process and begin to develop hypotheses about the particles, their size, and their behavior in water, which could then lead back to the concept of turbidity.

Driving Question

How does soil particle size affect turbidity?

Materials

- Sedimentator (see Chapter 3, Activity 9, and Figure 4.8)

- Copy of Soil Texture Triangle for Soil Composition Determination (see Figure 4.4, p. 72)

Procedure

1. Using the initial jar, which should be completely settled and ready for measurement, have students begin by diagramming and describing what they see. For example, at the top of the tube should be a clear layer of water followed by the soil separated into three distinct layers. The top layer, consisting of clay, is the finest of the three particles and takes the longest to settle. The remaining two layers, in order, are silt and sand.

2. Have students determine the percentage of clay, sand, and silt relative to the whole sample; this percentage is determined as shown in Table 4.4 (divide the value of each individual layer by the total value of all soil layers and multiply by 100). Have students locate the individual percentages on the texture chart (Figures 4.9, 4.10, and 4.11, p. 78); the point where all three intersect indicates the soil type of the sample.

FIGURE 4.8
Sedimentator

TABLE 4.4
Sample Measurement and Calculation of Soil Layers in a Sedimentator

Measurement of Soil Layers (total of all soil layers = 7.0 cm)	Calculation of Percentage of Each Soil Layer
Clay layer = 0.5 cm	Clay layer: 0.5/7.0 = 0.07 × 100 = 7%
Silt layer = 4.5 cm	Silt layer: 4.5/7.0 = 0.64 × 100 = 64%
Sand layer = 2.0 cm	Sand layer: 2.0/7.0 = 0.29 × 100 = 29%

FIGURE 4.9
Soil Texture Triangle—Clay

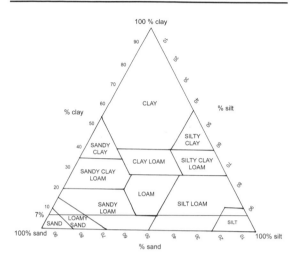

FIGURE 4.10
Soil Texture Triangle—Clay and Sand

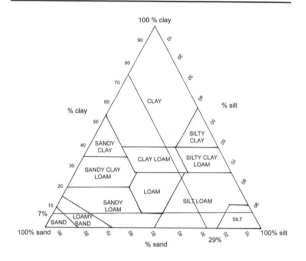

FIGURE 4.11
Soil Texture Triangle—Clay, Sand, and Silt

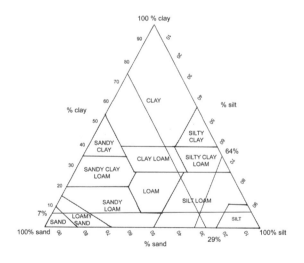

- Find the percentage of clay on the left side and draw a line to the right that is parallel to the triangle base. From Table 4.4 (p. 77) the amount of clay is 7%.

- Find the percentage of sand on the base and draw a line from the bottom up to the left, parallel to the right side. From Table 4.4 the amount of sand is 29%.

- Find the percentage of silt on the right side and draw a line from this side down toward the base, parallel to the left side. From Table 4.4 the amount of silt is 64%.

The resulting texture is *silt loam.*

3. This sample can then be compared with other samples being investigated. For each sample the type of soil can be determined using the process illustrated in steps 1 and 2.

4. Once the soil texture is identified for each sample, other types of investigation can be performed that relate to the overall properties of the soil. One of these properties, percolation of water through soil, will be the subject of Activity 3.

Think About

1. Which soil type settled first, and which settled last?

2. What accounts for these differences?

Activity 3. Percolation of Soil

In this activity we have students investigate the relationship between soil characteristics and two factors: the rate at which water moves through the soil (percolation rate) and the ability of soil to "hold" water (holding capacity). *Percolation* is defined as the movement of water through soil and is dependent on soil particle size and the space between particles. The activity involves testing a variety of soil samples, measuring the amount of water that drains through the soil, and determining the amount of water that is retained by the soil. In general the size of the spaces in the soil depends on the soil's texture; smaller spaces are found in soils with smaller particles, and larger spaces are found in soils with larger particles. Table 4.5 summarizes the relationship between soil texture and percolation and holding capacity of soil.

**TABLE 4.5
Relationship Between
Soil Texture and Percolation and
Holding Capacity**

Texture	Percolation	Water-Holding Capacity
Sand	Good	Poor
Silt	Medium	Medium
Clay	Poor	Good
Loam	Medium	Medium

Driving Question
How does soil type affect percolation rate?

Materials
(per group)
- Five damp (*not wet*) soil samples (damp soil better represents natural conditions): one sand, one clay (finely ground, nonclumping cat litter), one loam (top soil and/or potting soil), two others
- Five pie plates or paper plates
- Soil porosity and permeability tubes (Carolina Biological) or five plastic soda or water bottles; 20 oz. minimum for each bottle (remove labels)
- Percolation and Holding Capacity Data Sheet (p. 80)
- Cheesecloth, netting, and/or coffee filter (cheesecloth and netting are available at drugstores)
- Five 500 ml beakers (available from any science education supplier)
- Permanent marker (use low- or non-VOC marker)
- Ring stand (available from any science education supplier)
- Measuring cup or extra 500 ml beaker
- Stopwatch or wall clock with second hand
- Two 500 ml graduated cylinders (available from any science education supplier)
- Tap water or other source of water
- Scissors (Use caution, as scissors can cut skin.)
- Tape, rubber bands, or cable ties (enough to secure the cheesecloth to the container)
- Indirectly vented chemical splash goggles, aprons, and gloves

Procedure
1. Prepare percolation tubes by cutting the bottom out of each of the plastic bottles.

2. Wrap a piece of cheesecloth, netting, or coffee filter at the other end of the bottle.

Secure with tape, rubber band, and/or cable tie. Label each tube with soil type.

3. Secure the percolation tubes upside down so that the screen end faces into a beaker. Use ring stands or some other mechanism to keep the tube supported.

4. Label each beaker with the types of soil to be tested.

5. Place 1 cup (about 200–250 ml) of each soil in the appropriate tube. Be sure that each tube gets the same amount of soil.

6. Lightly shake the tube back and forth to settle soil to resemble natural conditions.

7. Slowly pour 100 ml of water, wait 30 seconds, and pour another 100 ml of water. Repeat until all 500 ml of water have been poured. Begin recording time when first 100 ml sample is poured.

8. Record the amount of time it takes for the first drip to occur.

9. Record the total amount of water collected in the beaker after five minutes on the data sheet in the "Volume Collected From Percolation" column.

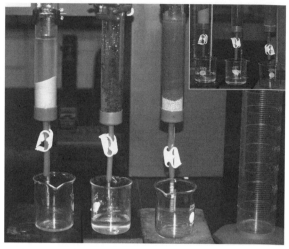

Soil Percolation

Water moving through columns containing soil samples to test percolation. From left: sand, topsoil, and cat litter (clay). Upper-right inset: After 5 minutes the amount of water (100 ml) that has drained from each sample can be seen.

10. If after five minutes no water has percolated, label that sample *impermeable*.

11. Determine and record the amount of water retained in the soil and record it on the data sheet. Repeat for each soil type. Wash hands with soap and water.

Percolation and Holding Capacity Data Sheet

Soil Type	Time First Drip Occurred (seconds)	Volume Collected From Percolation (ml)	Volume Retained in Soil After 5 Minutes	Soil Characteristics
1.				
2.				
3.				
4.				
5.				

Think About

1. Which sample had the fastest percolation time? Explain why.

2. Which sample had the slowest percolation time? Explain why.

3. Which sample drained the most amount of water? Explain why.

4. Which sample drained the least amount of water? Explain why.

5. Which sample had the highest holding capacity? Explain why.

6. Which sample had the lowest holding capacity? Explain why.

7. Describe the relationship between particle size and the percolation of water through the soil.

8. Describe the relationship between particle size and holding capacity of soil.

9. How can you account for missing water if the total water retained plus the total water collected does not equal the original 500 ml sample?

10. Which soil would you use to maximize plant growth? Explain your reasoning.

Activity 4. Soil Chemistry

In this activity we measure the basic chemical elements in soil. The point is to emphasize that all living organisms need nutrients to live and, thus, these nutrients should be found in the soil habitat. As an activity, soil chemistry examination can be conducted along with biodiversity analysis, which demonstrates the integrated nature of these content areas. A more detailed presentation of the importance of essential nutrients is found in Chapter 5.

FIGURE 4.12
Soil Test Kits

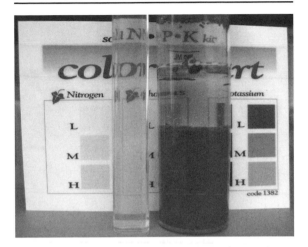

Soil test kits are simple to use and can be a good visual for students learning about the soil environment. In the tube on the left the color of the solution is compared with the color chart. In the tube on the right the soil sample has settled, allowing for the liquid on top to be tested.

Driving Question

Which chemicals are present in soil?

Materials

- Soil test kit (see Figure 4.12; these kits can be found in most garden stores and generally test for nitrogen, potassium, and phosphorous; we use the LaMotte kit used by the GLOBE [Global Learning and Observations to Benefit the Environment] program)

- Soil Test Kit Results Data Sheet (p. 82)

- Distilled water

- Indirectly vented chemical splash goggles, gloves, and aprons

Soil Activities

Soil Test Kit Results Data Sheet

Nitrogen		Phosphorous		Potassium	
Low		Low		Low	
Medium		Medium		Medium	
High		High		High	

Procedure

Provide students with the following instructions:

Preparation of Clear Solution

1. Fill the round tube to the 30 ml line with distilled water.

2. Add 2 Floc-Ex tablets. Cap the tube and mix until the tablets have disintegrated.

3. Remove the cap and add one heaping teaspoon of soil.

4. Cap the tube and shake for one minute.

5. Let the tube stand until the soil settles to the bottom. The clear solution above the soil is what you will use to test for nitrogen, phosphorous, and potassium.

Nitrogen Test

1. Use the pipet to transfer the clear solution above the soil to a square test tube until it is filled to the shoulder.

2. Add one Nitrate WR CTA tablet. Cap and mix until the tablet disintegrates.

3. Wait five minutes for the color to develop. Compare the pink color with the nitrogen color chart and mark the correct box on your data sheet.

Phosphorous Test

1. Use the pipet to transfer 25 drops of the clear solution above the soil to a square test tube.

2. Fill the tube to the shoulder with distilled water.

3. Add one phosphorous tablet. Cap and mix until the tablet disintegrates.

4. Wait five minutes for the color to develop. Compare the blue color to the phosphorous color chart and mark the correct box on your data sheet.

Potassium Test

1. Use the pipet to transfer the clear solution above the soil to a square test tube until it is filled to the shoulder.

2. Add one potassium tablet. Cap and mix until the tablet disintegrates.

3. Compare the cloudiness of the solution in the test tube with the potassium color chart. Hold the tube over the black boxes in the left column and compare it with the shaded boxes in the right column. Mark the correct box on your data sheet. Wash hands with soap and water after completing activities.

Think About

1. What nutrients were present in your soil sample?

2. Why might it be important for those nutrients to be found there?

3. Is there a link between nutrients found in soil and the biodiversity of that soil sample?

Activity 5. The Living Soil or Winogradsky Column

What does a Russian scientist named Sergei Winogradsky have to do with soil study? He was a microbiologist who specialized in the micro-organisms that inhabit soil and found a simple way of getting them to display themselves so that they could be viewed with the naked eye. He used a clear cylinder of soil and other components to encourage the growth of unseen bacteria, resulting in a display of colors produced by the bacteria over a period of time under the right conditions; this cylinder is known today as a Winogradsky column (Figure 4.13). This activity makes an excellent long-term inquiry in the classroom and requires almost no maintenance

FIGURE 4.13
Winogradsky Column

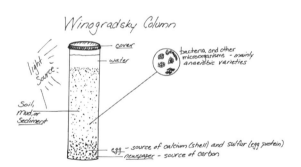

to be successful. In addition, this is a good way to make connections to our chapter on biodiversity (Chapter 6). An interesting part of this is that students can be taught that plants are not the only things that photosynthesize—some microbes do so also.

The construction of a Winogradsky column is simple and will engage students in a variety of skills. It can also be a messy endeavor, so prepare properly.

Driving Question

How can you demonstrate that soil is an environment for microbial life?

Materials

(per group of two or three students)

- A clear plastic tube (column) at least 12–24 inches in height and at least 2 inches in diameter (a 2-liter soda bottle will work well)

- A sample of soil or sediment from a pond or other aquatic environment, enough to fill the tube about 2 inches from the top

- A hard-boiled egg yolk or a raw egg (a source of sulfur; see Figure 4.14), a tablespoon or two of chalk dust (a source of calcium), and a sheet of newspaper (a

FIGURE 4.14
Winogradsky Column Showing Eggs

source of carbon); the ingredients and amounts will vary depending on the size of the column and your experimental setup

- Spring water or de-chlorinated water for making mud from the soil sample

Figure 4.15 Winogradsky Column Nine Years After Construction

- A lamp for a light source that does not produce too much heat (40–60 W) (Caution: Do not touch lamp—heat can burn skin.)

- A location to place the columns where they can remain undisturbed

- Plastic wrap to cover the top of tube

- Indirectly vented chemical splash goggles and aprons

Procedure
(Add ingredients in order indicated.)

1. Mix soil and sediment with water to make the soil wet but not runny.

2. Drop the raw egg (make sure it breaks) or hard-boiled yolk into the bottom of the container.

3. Add chalk dust.

4. Shred and add newspaper (no larger than 3 cm × 3 cm in size).

5. Add soil and sediment to within 8–10 cm from the top.

6. Slowly add water to fill the tube to within 1–2 cm from the top.

7. Cover the top of the tube with plastic wrap.

8. Place in an undisturbed area and expose to a light source (keep light at least 45 cm from the tube).

9. Monitor changes in the color and appearance of the soil and sediment over time. Wash hands with soap and water.

In Figure 4.15 note how the newspaper is still intact and can be read even though it has been exposed to water, mud, high sulfur content, and microbial action. One reason could be the lack of oxygen in the bottom portion of the column and the slow degradation of materials by mainly anaerobic bacteria.

Think About

1. For a true experiment set up another cylinder with soil and sediment only.

2. Think about and research why changes in the test cylinder occur.

3. Think about and research how nutrients in the soil play a role in stimulating the growth of microbes in the soil ecosystem

Wrap-Up

As you can see, soil studies involve a variety of hands-on activities and necessitate going outside where the soil is located. Getting students to think of soil beyond the notion of "dirt" and helping them understand the integrated role that living and nonliving factors play in soil formation is important for an overall understanding of the environment.

Resource List
Printed Material

Allaby, A., and M. Allaby, eds. 1999. *A dictionary of Earth sciences.* London: Oxford University Press.

Kesselheim, A. S., B. E. Slattery, S. H. Higgins, and M. R. Schilling. 1995. *Wow! The wonders of wetlands: An educator's guide.* St. Michaels, MD: Environmental Concern.

Lal, R., ed. 2002. *Encyclopedia of soil science.* New York: Marcel Dekker.

Websites

Discovery Education
http://school.discoveryeducation.com

Environmental Concern
www.wetland.org

Project Wet
www.projectwet.org

Soil Color (BioWorld Products)
www.adbio.com/science/soil/color.htm

U.S. Department of Agriculture (USDA), Natural Resources Conservation Service. 2007. *Soil survey manual,* Chapter 3: Examination and description of soils.
http://soils.usda.gov/technical/manual/contents/chapter3e.html

5

Energy and Nutrients

Many times throughout our day we see information about energy and nutrients but not necessarily in the context of the environment. Often these messages are in the form of advertising that promotes an "energy fix" with liquid consumables or nutrients that can be ingested in the form of a bar that comes in a neat package. But what is this energy and nutrient stuff? What is the composition of such materials? How does it relate to concepts in our environment? Inquiring minds (like yours) would like to know. To answer these questions and to help students explore the concepts of energy and nutrients, we need to go back to the fundamental connection of these concepts with the environment.

A Content Primer
What Is Energy?

The primary source of energy in the majority of terrestrial and aquatic ecosystems is light energy from the Sun. As a resource energy is a necessity for living organisms to do "work" and in the case of plants to manufacture food (glucose or sugar). Although sunlight that powers ecosystems is the most widely used example of an energy source, other examples include fossil fuels, geothermal energy, and wind and water. All sources have in common the ability to provide a form of energy that can be used to generate electricity and fuel the production of sugar in green plants.

Topic: What Is Energy?

Go to: *www.scilinks.org*

Code: IO025

Topic: Sources of Energy

Go to: *www.scilinks.org*

Code: IO026

Energy and Nutrients

FIGURE 5.1
Electromagnetic Spectrum

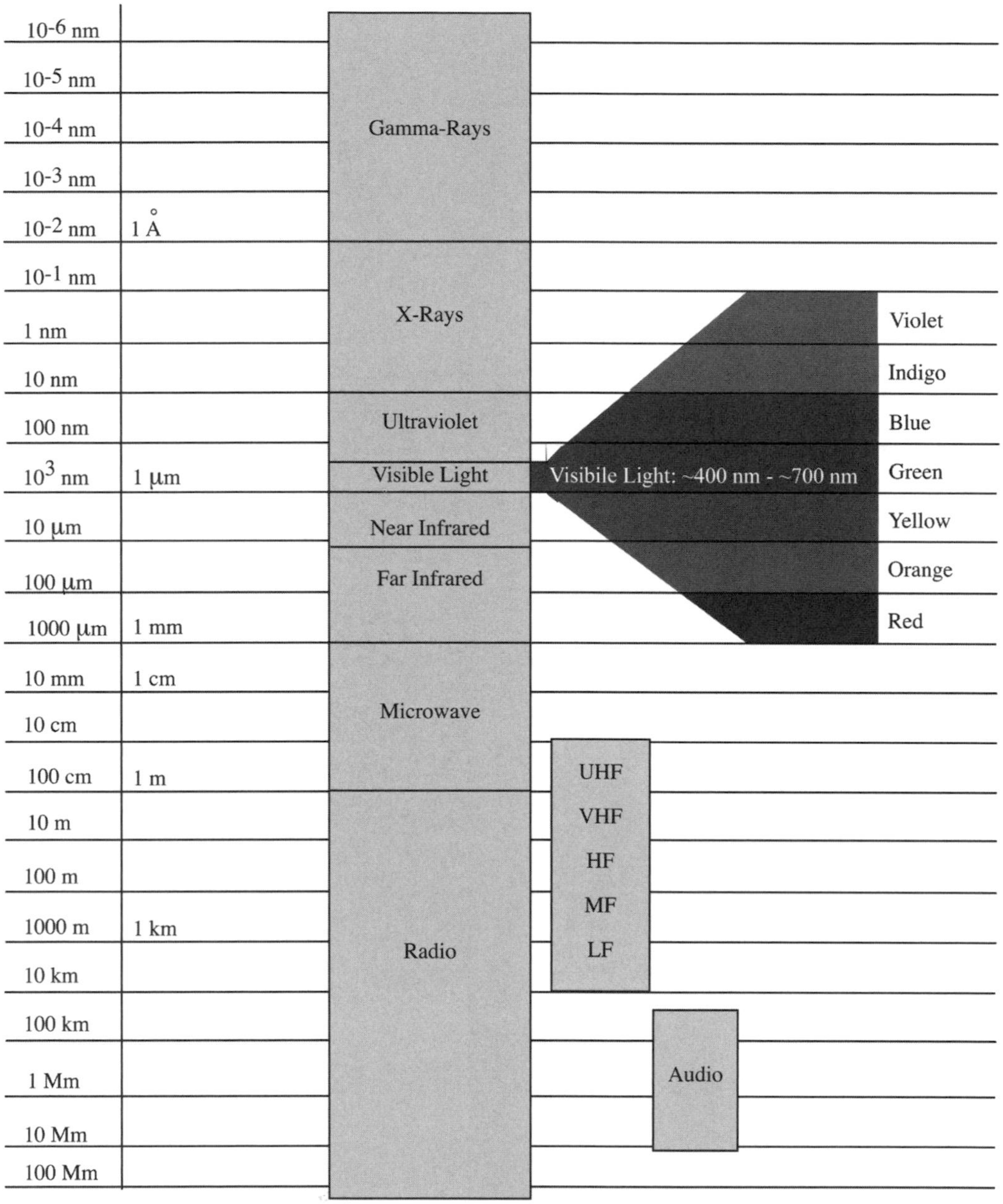

nm=nanometer, Å=angstrom, μm=micrometer, mm=millimeter,
cm=centimeter, m=meter, km=kilometer, Mm=Megameter

Source: http://lasp.colorado.edu/cassini/images/Electromagnetic%20Spectrum_noUVIS.jpg; reprinted with permission from University of Colorado, Boulder, Laboratory for Atmospheric and Space Physics.

Defining and Describing Light Energy

Light energy is part of the electromagnetic spectrum (EMS), a continuum (or scale) of wavelengths with various strengths and characteristics (see Figure 5.1). All the various parts of the EMS can be referred to as "waves" or "rays" and represent various forms of energy, from powerful, compact wavelengths at one end of the spectrum (including X-rays, which can be used to image our bones) to long, weak wavelengths at the other end (including radio waves, which help carry audio signals through our atmosphere). The part of the EMS that provides the necessary energy to most ecosystems is known as *visible light* (wavelength of 380–750 nanometers [nm]) and is sandwiched between ultraviolet rays (250 nm, stronger than visible light and responsible for that irritating sunburn) and infrared rays (10,000 nm, weaker than visible light and also represented by heat).

Importance of Light Energy

Energy from the Sun that powers most ecosystems is a form of light energy and enters an ecosystem through plants and algae because of their ability to "trap" or "capture" specific wavelengths of the visible light and transform them into a usable chemical form (sugar) through the process of *photosynthesis*. It is important to understand that unlike the water and nutrient cycles, which are also critical to ecosystems, energy *flows* in and out of ecosystems on a constant basis and is not considered a "cycle." It is also useful to know that while plants and algae trap energy from the Sun, only a small percentage (about 6%) of the total is actually used to convert sunlight to sugar. Part of the reason is that photosynthetic organisms use only some parts of the visible light spectrum, mainly absorbing red (680 nm) and blue (430 nm)

FIGURE 5.2
Glucose Molecule

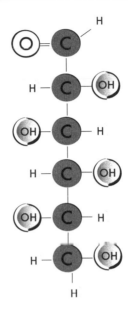

A simple two-dimensional illustration of a glucose molecule showing the number of carbon (C), hydrogen (H), and oxygen atoms (O). The = line represents a double bond between the C and O atoms and the – line represents a single bond between two atoms.

wavelengths for photosynthesis. Photosynthesis can be described as a process that can convert light energy into chemical energy (glucose; see Figure 5.2) and also serves to produce oxygen that is used by many organisms, including plants, in the process of aerobic (requiring oxygen) respiration. The basic components of the photosynthetic process are seen in Figure 5.3.

FIGURE 5.3
Basic Ingredients and Products of Photosynthesis

Ingredients IN	Products OUT
Light energy (Sun) + water + carbon dioxide ⟶	Sugar (e.g., glucose) + oxygen

Food Chains and Food Webs Based on Energy Flow

The fundamental concepts about energy make the connections between energy in an ecosystem and how it flows from the Sun, to plants and algae, and ultimately to animals, bacteria, and other organisms that consume these living things in a food web. As energy is transferred in an ecosystem, we assign names to the role of the organisms involved in the transfer. Plants, algae, and even some bacteria called cyanobacteria are involved in *energy production* and are called *producers,* like the ferns in Figure 5.4. Other organisms that *eat* or *decompose* living things are known as *consumers,* like the northern red salamander in Figure 5.5, or *decomposers,* like the millipede in Figure 5.6, bacteria, or the bracket fungus in Figure 5.7.

Aside from knowing the flow of energy, it is helpful to have a general understanding of the amount of energy transferred from producer to consumer and from consumer to consumer in the progression of energy through the food chain or web. Using a simple food chain as a model (Figure 5.8), we find that moss and algae (producers) successfully transform about 6% of the light energy available from the Sun into glucose. In turn the snail (a consumer) gains approximately 0.6% of that available energy

FIGURE 5.4
Ferns

FIGURE 5.5
Northern Red Salamander

FIGURE 5.6
Millipede

FIGURE 5.7
Bracket Fungus

from the moss and algae, the frog (a consumer) gains 0.06% of the energy from the snail, and the snake (a consumer) gains 0.006% of the energy from the frog. Notice that in each transfer a considerable amount of energy is lost (about a tenfold decrease). Most of the energy is lost as heat through activities of the organisms and cannot be recovered. On average only 10% of the available energy is passed on to the consumer in the food chain or web. It is amazing that what seems to be so little energy and poor efficiency has the ability to power an ecosystem properly.

Algae, not land plants, account for 30%–50% of all the oxygen on Earth through photosynthesis and span the globe through their growth in freshwater and marine environments. It is important to distinguish them and their role in the photosynthesizing process.

Exceptions to Photosynthesis

While the primary source of energy for a majority of ecosystems comes from the Sun, there are other recently discovered ecosystems that are thriving in the deep ocean. Ancient single-

FIGURE 5.8
Diagram of Transfer of Energy in a Food Chain

6% from the Sun
to the moss

.06% from the snail to
the frog

.006% from the frog
to the snake

0.6% from the moss to the snail

A simple food chain diagram illustrating the transfer (flow) of energy from the Sun and then sequentially from one organism to another; included are moss, snail, frog, and water snake.

FIGURE 5.9
Champagne Vent Near the Northern Mariana Islands in the Pacific Ocean

Source: http://oceanexplorer.noaa.gov/explorations/04fire/logs/april12/media/champagne_vent.html

celled microorganisms, known as *archaea*, convert chemicals (e.g., hydrogen sulfide, methane) coming from the seeps and cracks in the ocean floor (hydrothermal vents; see Figure 5.9) into usable energy through a process called *chemosynthesis* (see Figure 5.10). These deep-sea vent environments support incredible diversity of life, and exploration has resulted in the discovery of hundreds of new species. More information is available at the following websites:

- *http://oceanexplorer.noaa.gov* (National Oceanic and Atmospheric Administration [NOAA] Ocean Explorer program)

- *http://ocean.si.edu/ocean_hall* (the Sant Ocean Hall at the Smithsonian Museum of Natural History)

- *http://www.vims.edu/bridge* (the Bridge ocean resource education center)

Why Chemistry, and What Are Nutrients?

In the study of living things the main elements necessary for life are called macro- and micro-nutrients. *Micronutrients* are so called "because they are needed only in minuscule amounts, these substances are the 'magic wands' that enable the body to produce enzymes, hormones and other substances essential for proper growth and development…Iodine, vitamin A and iron are most important in global public health terms" (World Health Organization). *Macronutrients* are those that organisms consume and need in relatively large quantities. These elements include carbon, hydrogen, nitrogen, oxygen, phosphorous, and sulfur and are consumed through the food we eat (protein, fat, and carbohydrates) (University of Illinois at Urbana-Champaign, McKinley Health Center).

In water and soil studies, assessing the levels of certain macronutrients provides a foundational understanding of the quality of water and soil samples. In soil studies, the three elements generally tested for are nitrogen, phosphorous, and potassium. In water quality analysis, nitrogen and phosphorous are the most important nutrients to measure and are often considered the

FIGURE 5.10
Basic Ingredients and Products of Chemosynthesis

Ingredients IN	Products OUT
Compounds (e.g., hydrogen sulfide) + carbon dioxide + water ⟶	Sugar (e.g., glucose) + sulfate chemical compounds

Energy and Nutrients

"limiting factors," nutrients that are necessary for life and need to remain in balance for proper ecosystem function. Moderation is the key to quality of life and, similar to the delicate balance of pH, an excess of nitrogen and phosphorous can pose hazards to the stability of a system.

Essential Elements

The elements (macronutrients) that are essential for all organisms to live are outlined in Table 5.1 (p. 94). Each element plays a specific role in the chemical processes that support life. Having a general understanding of element sources and their role in the environment as well as their connection to life is a major step toward eliminating misconceptions in science and developing a holistic understanding of the health of an ecosystem.

Essential Cycles

The following sections explain and illustrate three important nutrient cycles: nitrogen, carbon, and phosphorous. The information is presented in two forms: as a diagram of each cycle and as an associated table summarizing the major reactions within the cycle. Each table includes the terms *catalysts*, *reactants*, and *products*. *Catalysts* are biotic and/or abiotic factors that initiate or regulate a reaction. *Reactants* are the components that are being acted upon by the catalyst, and the *products* are the end results of the reaction.

Nitrogen

Nitrogen gas (N_2) accounts for about 78% of atmospheric composition. Nitrogen is a key component of living things and plays a key role

in the structure of proteins and nucleic acids found in nearly all cells, tissues, and organs. Nitrogen enters an ecosystem through the process of fixation, moderated mainly by a variety of species of bacteria. *Fixation* is defined as the conversion of nitrogen from an inert form (N_2) to a usable compound (ammonia NH_3) by bacteria. This process makes nitrogen available for uptake by plants initiating the nitrogen cycle that connects plant, animal, and microbial life (see Figure 5.11 and Table 5.2, p. 95). In the uptake (or assimilation) process, plants that have symbiotic relationships with bacteria are supplied with ammonium from the nodules; other plants absorb nitrate from the soil via their root hairs. These are then reduced to nitrite ions and then ammonium ions for incorporation into amino acids, and hence protein, which forms part of the plants or animals that eat them.

FIGURE 5.11
The Nitrogen Cycle

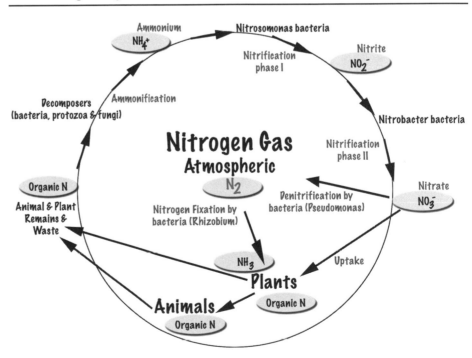

Energy and Nutrients

TABLE 5.1
Key to Important Elements for Life

Element	Use	Concerns/Problems
Carbon • Main organic element • Found in macronutrients (proteins, lipids, and carbohydrates) and nucleic acids	• Building block for glucose $C_6H_{12}O_6$: the simple sugar product of photosynthesis. Carbon chains form backbone of other organic compounds. • $C_6H_{12}O_6$: Used in cellular respiration for all energy-requiring processes (conversion to ATP, energy source)	• Elevated CO_2 levels may be linked to climate change
Hydrogen • Found in water • Found in macronutrients (proteins, lipids, and carbohydrates) and nucleic acids	• Plants use H_2O in the process of photosynthesis. Hydrogen is used to make carbohydrates and other compounds. • Animals digest simple sugars and other compounds (carbohydrates, lipids, and proteins) to supply energy.	• Needed for water and for building and breaking down complex organic compounds (respiration)
Nitrogen • Found in nucleic acids (DNA/RNA): thymine, cytosine, adenine, and guanine are nitrogen bases for DNA, and uracil replaces guanine in RNA • Found in proteins (amino acids), including enzymes for all body reactions	• Nitrifying process: Ammonia and ammonia compounds (NH_3) → nitrite (NO_2-) → nitrate (NO_3-) by nitrifying bacteria → taken up by plants→ consumed by animals • Lightning also nitrifies N_2 in atmosphere.	• Acts as a nutrient; too much can cause excess plant growth in aquatic systems (nutrient loading)
Oxygen • Found in atmosphere as gas molecule O_2 • Found in water, proteins, lipids, carbohydrates, and nucleic acids)	• Animals, plants, and other organisms: used in respiration as O_2 to make energy • Plants: used in photosynthesis as CO_2	• Needed for cellular respiration by both plants and animals
Phosphorous • Found in rocks, proteins, lipids, and nucleic acids	• Leached from rocks and absorbed into plants as H_2PO_4- • Building block for ATP, a universal energy molecule	• Important for respiration and photosynthesis • Acts as a nutrient; too much can cause excess plant growth in aquatic systems (nutrient loading)
Sulfur • Found in proteins (amino acids)	• Used as building block of protein (amino acids)	• Crucial for bridge/link to form complex proteins (that have three-dimensional structure) • Too much in form of hydrogen sulfide (H_2S) can be a concern for aquatic organisms

ATP = adenosine triphosphate

Energy and Nutrients

The Relationship of Carbon and Oxygen

Carbon is the backbone of all the organic compounds found in nature (e.g., sugar and fats) and is also found in inorganic forms such as carbon dioxide (CO_2; about 0.036% of atmospheric gas). Carbon can be found in a number of forms and can enter into an ecosystem in a variety of ways. One of the most common ways is through plants by photosynthesis, in which CO_2 is converted into a carbon compound of glucose (sugar) (see Figure 5.12 and Table 5.3, pp. 96–97). Carbon can also enter into aquatic and marine ecosystems by becoming soluble in water and then becoming associated with other elements to form compounds like carbonic acid or be used by organisms to form shells in the form of calcium carbonate ($CaCO_3$). It can also be found as ions called bicarbonates (HCO_3^-) from weathered rocks and will enter ecosystems through this path. Carbon typically gets back into the form of CO_2 from the process of respiration by living things and reenters the atmosphere or aquatic ecosystem.

As presented in the content primer of Chapter 3, oxygen (O_2) accounts for approximately

Topic: Nitrogen Cycle
Go to: *www.scilinks.org*
Code: IO031

Topic: Carbon Cycle
Go to: *www.scilinks.org*
Code: IO032

TABLE 5.2
The Major Reactions in the Nitrogen Cycle

Reaction	Catalysts	Reactants	Products	Product Traits
Ammonification	Bacteria, fungi, protozoans; moisture	Decomposing animals and plants; animal waste	Ammonium, NH_4^+	Toxic to many forms of life (especially in aquatic environment)
Nitrification phase I	Bacteria, *Nitrosomonas*	Ammonium, NH_4^+, oxygen	Nitrite, NO_2^-	Toxic to many forms of life (especially in aquatic environment)
Nitrification phase II	Bacteria, *Nitrobacter*	Nitrite, NO_2^-, oxygen	Nitrate, NO_3^-	Nontoxic to many forms of life, source of nutrients for many plants
Denitrification	Bacteria, *Pseudomonas* species	Nitrate, NO_3^-, oxygen	Nitrogen gas, N_2	Most abundant gas in our atmosphere, nontoxic, provides N source
Nitrogen fixation	Bacteria, *Rhizobium, Azotobacter,* or lightning	Nitrogen gas, N_2, mainly anaerobic (no oxygen required), water as a source of H	Free ammonia, NH_3	Source for plants to use as a nutrient and building block for other compounds like proteins
Uptake	Plants; no other intermediary needed	Nitrate, NO_3^-	Plant structures and proteins	Varied types of structural plant components that are a cache for nitrogen

FIGURE 5.12
The Carbon Cycle

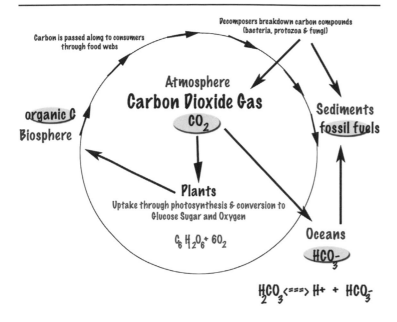

21% of the gas in our atmosphere, and in water this gas is dissolved and is referred to as *dissolved oxygen*, or DO (see Chapter 3 for more detail). Measuring the DO of a water sample is crucial for an overall understanding of the quality of that sample and the ability of life to survive in that water.

Phosphorous

Phosphorous has its origin mainly in rocks and through the process of weathering and erosion enters into a cycle in an ecosystem (see Figure 5.13). Because it is highly reactive, phosphorous is usually found as an ion or a compound with other elements. Once it is released into an ecosystem (e.g., as a phosphate ion, PO_4^{-3}), it is converted to a usable form for plants through absorption from soils or water. Then it becomes a key component in cell membranes, nucleic acids, and an energy-containing compound known as ATP (adenosine triphosphate), which is important in respiration (see Table 5.4, p. 98).

Tying It All Together: Nutrient Loading and Water Quality

In balanced aquatic systems the essential nutrients are maintained in relative equilibrium. Natural events, however, can lead to nutrient loading, which can then impact the system's overall quality, including turbidity. In Chapter 3 we defined *turbidity* as the relative measure of the cloudiness of a body of water due to an increase in suspended substances in the water column, and we explained that these suspended particles can be both abiotic and biotic in nature. For example, there can be a return of nutrients and sediments to the system after a forest fire, or nutrients can upwell from deeper to shallower waters; both of these situations can lead to excessive nutrient loads that harm the aquatic ecosystem.

More commonly, however, human influences result in excessive nutrient loading. Nitrogen and phosphorous in the form of land-based agricultural fertilizers or improperly treated sewage can lead to an overload of these elements in an aquatic system. While essential for life, a

FIGURE 5.13
The Phosphorous Cycle

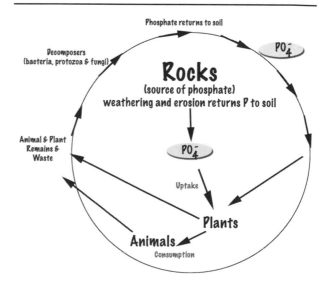

TABLE 5.3
The Major Reactions in the Carbon/Oxygen Cycle

Reaction	Catalysts	Reactants	Products	Product Traits
Photosynthesis in terrestrial and aquatic ecosystems	Sunlight catalyzes the conversion of inorganic C to organic C in plants.	CO_2 gas, H_2O, chlorophyll	Glucose sugar, $C_6H_{12}O_6$, and oxygen	Glucose sugar (organic C) is used as a universal energy source and catalyzes further conversion of carbon into proteins, fats, and nucleic acids when combined with other building blocks.
Transfer of organic carbon from plants to animals	Animals and enzymes	Glucose sugar, $C_6H_{12}O_6$, and oxygen	Energy (adenosine triphosphate [ATP]), CO_2, and H_2O	Energy (ATP) for work and growth. CO_2 is a waste product and H_2O is recycled.
Organic carbon breakdown through respiration, decomposition, and fermentation	Bacteria, fungi, and/or enzymes	Organic compounds carbohydrates, proteins, fats, nucleic acids from plant and animal matter, and water	CO_2 gas, water, heat, methane, and stored organic C compounds	Some carbon compounds will break down through a number of processes while others will become sequestered (fossil fuel, sediments). Once released they become part of the inorganic-organic cycling.
Inorganic carbon utilization in the ocean	pH conditions and the chemical equilibrium of reaction $H_2CO_3 \Leftrightarrow H^+ + HCO_3^-$ (bicarbonate)	Reduced forms of CO_2 like carbonic acid H_2CO_3 (from $CO_2 + H2O \Leftrightarrow H_2CO_3$)	Bicarbonate, hydrogen ions, and carbonic acid H_2CO_3	This chemical equilibrium in the ocean helps regulate the pH conditions and provide available carbon for the formation of calcium carbonate compounds for organisms.
Combustion of organic materials	Energy source	Fossil fuels, oxygen	CO_2 gas, water vapor, other SOx and NOx products	Combustion of fossil fuels plays a large role in the release of CO_2 gas, along with other products, in our world today.
Ocean surface warming	Temperature rise	Soluble CO_2 gas	CO_2 gas released into the atmosphere	Source of CO_2 gas released back into the carbon/oxygen cycle

Inside-Out: Environmental Science in the Classroom and the Field, Grades 3–8

TABLE 5.4
The Major Reactions in the Phosphorous Cycle

Reaction	Catalysts	Reactants	Products	Product Traits
Weathering from rocks and ocean sediments	Natural eroding forces in nature	Rocks containing phosphate compounds release PO_4^{-3}	PO_4^{-3} compounds ready for uptake	PO_4^{-3} is readily taken up by plants in both terrestrial and aquatic environments and is used for growth and a building block for nucleotides (in genetic material), as a stored energy source in cells (adenosine triphosphate [ATP]), and to build cell membranes and bones (calcium phosphate).
Consumption of plants by consumers	Enzymes	Plants containing PO_4^{-3}-based compounds	Cell membranes, nucleotides, and ATP	P becomes part of a stored energy source in cells and for building cell membranes and bones (calcium phosphate).
Decay of plants and animals	Bacteria, fungi, protists	Plant and animal decay and decomposition	Free compounds release PO_4^{-3}	Released PO_4^{-3} compounds are ready for uptake again or will become trapped in sediments or rock.

nutrient overload can cause a chain reaction that ultimately leads to extremely low oxygen concentrations and the death of many aquatic organisms. A generalized sequence follows:

1. The system sustains a nutrient overload (in the form of nitrogen and/or phosphorous).

2. The nutrient overload leads to an algal bloom (overgrowth of algae).

3. The algal bloom increases the turbidity of water and decreases light penetration to the bottom, which negatively impacts the growth of submerged aquatic vegetation.

4. The algae eventually exhaust the nutrient supply, leading to a *die-off*, or *crash* (die-offs also may be caused by a weather event, such as a thunderstorm).

5. The dead algae sink to the bottom and are decomposed through bacterial respiration, an aerobic process. (Aerobic respiration consumes oxygen and, thus, oxygen levels in the water are decreased.)

6. Reduced oxygen levels, initially through bacterial respiration, are termed *hypoxia* (O_2 levels below 5 parts per million [ppm]) or *anoxia* (O_2 levels below 0.5 ppm). Both conditions refer to very low levels of oxygen that can cause major die-offs among many organisms within a system.

In summary, the nutrient overload leads to a sequence of events that ultimately has disastrous effects on life within that aquatic system (see Figure 5.14).

FIGURE 5.14
The Impact of Nutrients in the Chesapeake Bay Ecosystem

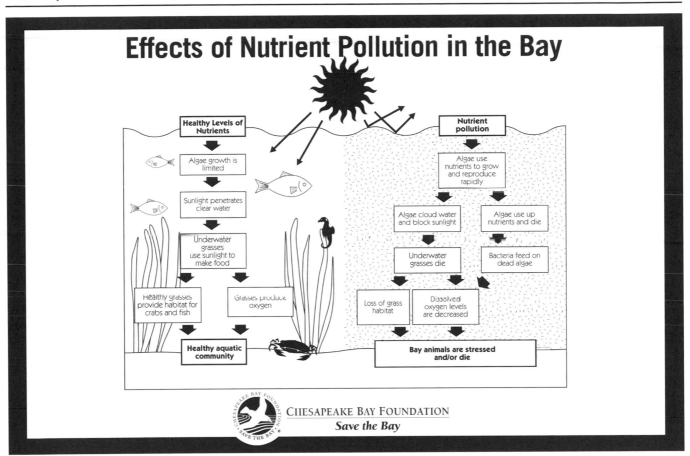

Source: Chesapeake Bay Foundation

5 Energy Activities

In each of the following activities, data can be collected and shared among the students or students can design their own experiments to explore simple, but important, concepts in energy.

ENERGY ACTIVITIES

Activity 1. Exploring How Light Source Affects Plant Growth

The exploration of energy can begin with simple activities that tie together the classroom, the local environment, and observation and inquiry skills. Growing plants with different kinds of light is one of the best activities and provides many links to basic science concepts and the process of science. By varying the type of light the plants are exposed to, differences in growth and development can be observed as long as all other conditions are similar (see Figure 5.15). This activity can be performed in a room with or without windows or other sources of constant light. The University of Illinois Extension Houseplants website provides simple information on home plant care (*http://urbanext.illinois.edu/houseplants*).

FIGURE 5.15
A Simple Setup Illustrating the Difference in Growth Between a Plant Exposed to Fluorescent Lighting (FL) and a Plant Exposed to Incandescent Lighting (IL)

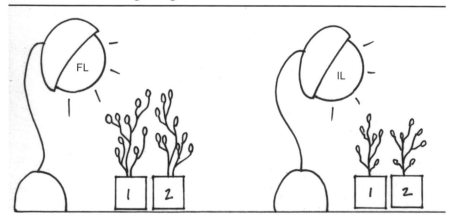

Driving Question
How can varying the type of light plants are exposed to affect their growth or development?

Materials
(ideally per group of two to three students)

- Two types of lights (e.g., standard household incandescent light vs. fluorescent light; available at lawn and garden centers or discount stores) (Caution: Do not touch lamp bulbs, as they can burn skin.)

- Two light timers (available at hardware stores, discount stores, or home improvement stores)

- Three plants (e.g., beans or peas, which can be grown from seeds, or any simple ornamental plants; seeds are available at lawn and garden centers)

- Digital camera

- An area of a room where the experiment can be set up and the lights and plants being tested can be separated from one another

Procedure
1. Take measurements and pictures of the plants as a baseline for comparison. If using plants from seeds, wait until they reach a reasonable height (10–15 cm should do) and/or until secondary leaves are growing.

2. Set one plant under your first light setup (e.g., fluorescent light).

3. Set the second plant under your other light setup (e.g., grow light). If windows are available, set the third plant on the windowsill.

4. Provide each plant the same amount of water and equal exposure to its particular light source.

5. Continue monitoring changes in plant growth through observation and photographic record of the plants' growth over time (2–3 weeks).

6. Have each group graph their growth results over time to determine a pattern in growth relative to light source.

7. Create a larger data set (full-class data) by constructing a daily class chart for the height of each plant. At the end of each day, calculate the average height for each group of plants. Use these data to compare individual group data with whole-class results.

8. Save plants for additional experiments on the effects of nutrients, salt, gravity, or other variables students want to test.

Think About

1. What do the graphs tell you about the relationship between plant growth and a particular type of light source?

2. Why is it important that, except for light, we maintain all other abiotic factors?

3. How might you explain any differences in plant growth?

4. If you were growing plants at home, maybe for a vegetable or flower garden, which type of light would you use?

Activity 2. Exploring Energy Through Evaporation

Energy can also be examined by looking at how long the process of evaporation of water takes under varying temperatures.

Driving Question

How does temperature affect evaporation rate?

Materials

- One hot plate (available from science education suppliers). Use caution when working with hot plates, as they can burn skin.

- Two Pyrex-type beakers of equal volume (Do not use jars, as they can shatter from heating.)

- Water

- Nonmercury stick thermometers (available from science education suppliers)

- Indirectly vented chemical splash goggles and aprons

Procedure

1. Set up two beakers of equal amounts of water. Mark the original level of the water on the jars, or use beakers with graduated measurements.

2. Heat one sample on the hot plate; leave the other sample alone (not heated).

3. Throughout the class period continue to heat one sample, but not the other. As time passes, the water level can be marked or observed.

4. Students should observe and record what happens to the amount of water in each container by the end of the class period and by the end of the school day.

5. Following their observations, provide opportunity for student discourse. Questions from students should drive the conversation. "Where did the water go?" "How hot is the water?" "Why is one slower than the other?"—these are the types of questions that should be posed by students and can be explained by them as well with encouragement.

Think About

1. Which causes evaporation rates to increase: colder or warmer temperatures?

2. What happens to the water molecules when they evaporate?

Activity 3. Exploring Energy Through Heat and Circulation

Topic: Heat Energy

Go to: *www.scilinks.org*

Code: IO033

Energy can be explored by using water, food coloring, and a heat source (hot plate). This is a great way to introduce the concept of energy (heat in this case) and how it is able to move the water molecules around in the jar. (It is also a great way to introduce circulation to students, since that is how the dye will move.) Figures 5.16 and 5.17 show what happens when you mix food coloring in cold water versus hot water.

Driving Question

How does heat energy affect the movement of a molecule of water?

Materials

- Source of cold water (approx. 10° C) and hot water (approx. 40° C) from the tap (a hot plate is optional for hot water, and refrigerated water is optional for cold water)

- Two beakers of equal volume

- Blue food coloring (available in the baking goods aisle of the supermarket)

- Nonmercury stick thermometers (available from science education suppliers)

- Indirectly vented chemical splash goggles and aprons

Procedure

1. Place beakers of cold water and hot water next to each other. Let the water in the jars

FIGURE 5.16
Movement of Food Coloring in Cold Tap Water

Two beakers used to demonstrate the movement of blue food coloring in cold tap water from the initial drop (*left*) and after five minutes (*right*).

FIGURE 5.17
Movement of Food Coloring in Hot Tap Water

Two beakers used to demonstrate the movement of blue food coloring in hot tap water from the initial drop (*left*) and after five minutes (*right*).

settle so it is not visibly moving. Be careful with hot plates and hot water, as they can burn skin.

2. Record the temperature of each sample.

3. Add 2 drops of blue food coloring to each beaker.

4. Have students make and record observations about what food coloring does as it enters the water and then how it looks after five minutes.

Think About

1. How do your observations of the food coloring differ between the samples?

2. What is the relationship between the temperature of the water and the appearance of the food coloring in each of the samples?

NUTRIENTS ACTIVITIES

Activity 4. Chemical Water Quality Analysis

Chemical water quality analysis of essential nutrients can be accomplished with inexpensive commercially available water test kits; we like the CHEMetrics test kits for ease of use (*www. chemetrics.com*). Figure 5.18 shows a CHEMetrics kit used to test DO of a stream. For stream analysis we use the Stream Water Quality Data Sheet (p. 104). For deeper water, when we want a top and bottom sample, and if we are adding salinity to our tests, we use the Water Quality Data Sheet for Deep and/or Brackish Water (p. 105).

Chemical testing and analysis are relatively straightforward. Most test kits give you a key that indicates what the measured level indicates regarding water quality. If you cannot find these values, then contact your state department of environmental conservation. Table 5.5 (p. 106)

FIGURE 5.18
A CHEMetrics Dissolved Oxygen (DO) Test Kit Provides a Simple Way to Obtain Quick DO Levels.

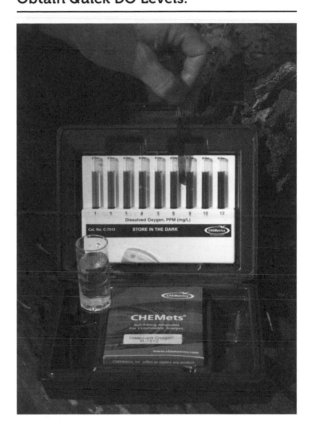

also offers information that students can use to determine the relative quality of the water at the sample site. For this activity, be sure to have appropriate ventilation.

Driving Question

What are the advantages and limitations of water quality analysis?

Materials

(per group, except as noted)

- Water quality test kit (available from CHEMetrics, *www.chemetrics.com*)

- Data sheets (laminated if possible)

Stream Water Quality Data Sheet

Location site: _____ Date:_____

School: _____

	Measurement (Value)		General Conclusion (Excellent / Good / Fair / Poor)
Dissolved oxygen (ppm and % saturation)	_____ ppm	_____ % sat.	
Nitrate (ppm)			
Phosphate (ppm)			
pH			
Temperature (°C)			
Turbidity (depth in cm using turbidity tube			
Appearance (description)			

Water Quality Data Sheet for Deep and/or Brackish Water

Location site: _____   Date:_____

	Depth A Top		Depth C Bottom (_____ meters)	
Dissolved oxygen (ppm and % saturation)	_____ ppm	_____ % sat.	_____ ppm	_____ % sat.
Nitrate (ppm)				
Phosphate (ppm)				
pH				
Turbidity (using Secchi disk; how clear is the water?)				
Salinity (% dissolved solids)				
Temperature (ºC)				
Appearance (description)				

TABLE 5.5
Student "Cheat Sheet" for Water Quality Analysis: What the Data Indicate

Test	What It Measures	Result From Test Kit and Equivalent Ranking	Comments
pH	Acidity of water	pH 5 and below = 1 (poor) pH 6 = 3 (good) pH 7 = 4 (excellent) pH 8 = 3 (good) pH 9 and above = 1 (poor)	Most living organisms live best in a pH range between 6.2 and 8.2. A pH of 7 is considered ideal.
Dissolved oxygen (DO) and % saturation	Amount of oxygen dissolved in water and available for respiration	(Determine ppm and temperature in °C and then use % saturation chart to find value.) 91%–110% saturation = 4 (excellent) 71%–90% saturation = 3 (good) 51%–70% saturation = 2 (fair) < 50% saturation = 1 (poor)	General guidelines: 5 mg/l (ppm) Hypoxia < 5 ppm Anoxia < 0.5 ppm O_2 is more soluble and is consumed more slowly in cold water. Thus, it is less soluble and consumed more quickly in warm water, which leads to decay, respiration, and O_2 reduction.
Nitrate*	Nutrient used for DNA and amino acids for proteins	0 ppm = 4 (excellent) 1–4 ppm = 3 (good) 5–9 ppm = 2 (fair) 10 ppm or above = 1 (poor)	Acts as a nutrient; comes from fertilizer; too much = too much algae growth in aquatic systems
Phosphate*	Nutrient for adenosine triphosphate (ATP): energy from respiration, from breakdown of glucose	0–0.03 ppm = 4 (excellent) 0.1 ppm and above = 1 (poor) (see HACH Company website, *www.h2ou.com*)	Very important for respiration and photosynthesis, but too much leads to too much algae growth
Salinity	Amount of dissolved salts	Freshwater 0.25–0.5 ppt = 3 (good) Brackish 0.5–17 ppt = 3 (good) Ocean 17–37 ppt = 3 (good)	Salinity determines the types of organisms living in water: higher salt, more saltwater organisms; less salt, more freshwater organisms.
Temperature	Temperature in degrees Celsius (0°C = 32°F; 20°C = 68°F)	Ambient temperature ranges vary for different species, but generally temperature plays a key role in the amount of DO available.	Temperature affects the amount of DO in the water. Increasing water temperature will result in less DO and can stress living organisms.
Turbidity	Amount of suspended (living and nonliving) solids in water	Secchi depth using Secchi disk (pond, lake, river, bay, ocean) or turbidity tube (river and/or stream); this is a relative measurement: • Disk disappears at deeper depth = lower turbidity • Disk disappears at shallower depth = higher turbidity	Determines water clarity. Higher turbidity decreases light penetration and thus prevents plants from photosynthesizing.

*As nutrients, excess nitrate and phosphorous levels in water can lead to an increase in algae growth, which eventually will lead to an algae die-off and a decrease in oxygen. However, the Canadian Water Quality Guideline clearly indicates the difficulty of linking a single value of nitrate or phosphorous to water quality (see *www.ec.gc.ca/ceqg-rcqe/English/Html/GAAG_Nitrate_WQG.cfm* and *www.ec.gc.ca/ceqg-rcqe/English/Html/GAAG_Phosphorus_WQG.cfm*).

FIGURE 5.19
Percent Saturation of Oxygen

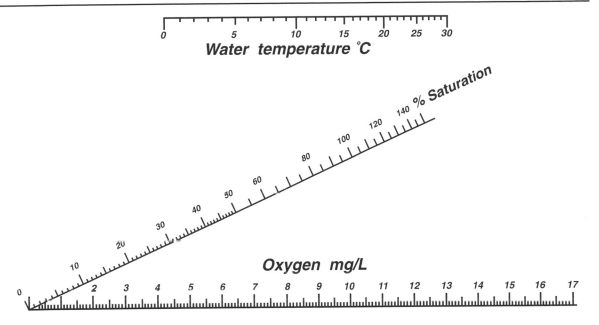

- Laminated instructions for each test (if possible)

- Oxygen percent saturation chart (Figure 5.19; review Chapter 3 if necessary)

- Clipboards

- Pencil (one per person)

- Nonmercury stick thermometer (available from science education suppliers)

- Waste container (small bucket)

- Indirectly vented chemical splash goggles and aprons

Procedure

1. Organize the class into teams: TEAM DO, TEAM pH, TEAM NITRATE, and so on.

2. Have the teams read the test kit instructions beforehand.

3. Have the teams conduct each test in the classroom using tap water as a trial run.

4. Go in the field and have the teams conduct tests. Briefly review the results as a team in the field.

5. Back in the classroom collect full class data to use for discussion. Wash hands with soap and water.

6. For future tests have teams rotate so that they test different parameters.

Think About

1. What general statements can be made about water quality relative to data collected?

2. Explain why these data may only be considered a "snapshot" of the quality of the study site.

Topic: Aquatic Ecosystems

Go to: www.scilinks.org

Code: IO034

Activity 5. Tying It All Together: Nutrient Loading, Turbidity, and Water Quality. What's the Story?

This activity uses Figure 5.14 (The Impact of Nutrients in the Chesapeake Bay Ecosystem [p. 99]) from earlier in this chapter, but here we cover up the text in the diagram and ask students to complete the story. While this activity is probably seen more as an assessment of student understanding, we find that this task is a good application of knowledge as students synthesize all the pieces of the effects of nutrients on an aquatic system.

Driving Question

How do nutrients impact a body of water?

Materials

- Figure 5.14 (for reference)

- Figure 5.20 (fill-in-the-blanks version of Figure 5.14)

FIGURE 5.20
Fill-in-the-Blanks Version of Figure 5.14, The Impact of Nutrients in the Chesapeake Bay Ecosystem

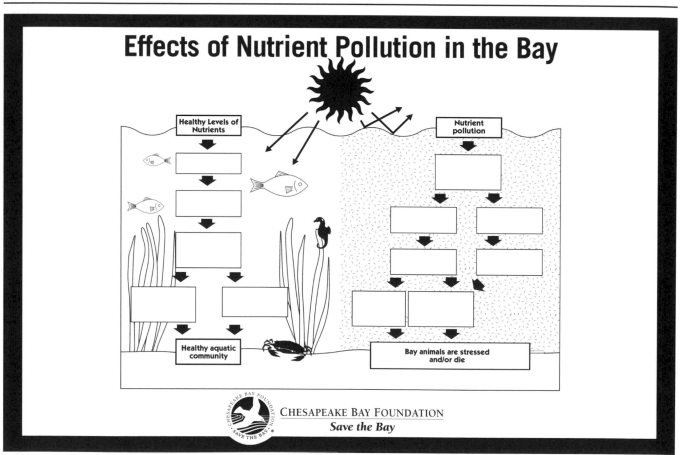

Source: Chesapeake Bay Program

Procedure

Ask students to fill in the boxes of Figure 5.20, or cover various text boxes of Figure 5.14 and ask students to complete the story.

Think About

Discuss the implications of the information in the boxes on the quality of an aquatic ecosystem.

Wrap-Up

Understanding the role that energy and nutrients play in the sustainability of an ecosystem is fundamental in studying the outside world. All living things need energy and essential nutrients, but an excess can cause a variety of problems, whether in an aquatic system or in the human population. As we move to the next chapter, on biodiversity, and complete our presentation of the content in the study of the environment, you should begin to see the integrated nature of all topics herein and how each is essential to outdoor learning.

Resource List
Websites

Canadian Water Quality Guideline
Nitrate:
www.ec.gc.ca/ceqg-rcqe/English/Html/GAAG_Nitrate_WQG.cfm

Phosphorous:
www.ec.gc.ca/ceqg-rcqe/English/Html/GAAG_Phosphorus_WQG.cfm

HACH Company (information about water testing)
www.h2ou.com

LaMotte Company (science education and water-based curricula)
www.lamotte.com/pages/edu/5419.html
www.lamotte.com/pages/edu/curricul/index.html

National Oceanic and Atmospheric Administration, Ocean Explorer program
http://oceanexplorer.noaa.gov

Smithsonian Institution, National Museum of Natural History, Sant Ocean Hall
http://ocean.si.edu/ocean_hall

University of Illinois at Urbana-Champaign, McKinley Health Center ("Macronutrients: The Importance of Carbohydrate, Protein, and Fat")
www.mckinley.illinois.edu/Handouts/macronutrients.htm

University of Illinois Extension ("Houseplants")
http://urbanext.illinois.edu/houseplants

Virginia Institute of Marine Science
www.vims.edu/bridge

World Health Organization ("Micronutrients")
www.who.int/nutrition/topics/micronutrients/en

6

Biodiversity

Finding an organism that you have never seen before is a thrilling experience even if it is not something exotic or rare. Students exposed to the exploration of local biodiversity will no doubt have many "first-time sightings," especially if their experiences in the environment have been limited. In fact, one of the authors (J. Adam Frederick) can recount many of his initial observations of organisms that he has observed, from salamanders to insects, with equal excitement and detail—even as an adult. In 2009 he found a type of salamander that he had never seen before in a stream on the Blue Ridge Parkway near Asheville, North Carolina. With the enthusiasm of a third-grader he used both field guides and the internet to make an identification of this organism as a variety of dusky salamander (Figure 6.1 [p. 112]; see also *www.herpsofnc.org*).

This same enthusiasm exists within your students—all they need is the exposure and some opportunities to make observations in the field

Biodiversity

FIGURE 6.1
Dusky Salamander

SCI LINKS.
THE WORLD'S A CLICK AWAY

Topic: Biodiversity
Go to: *www.scilinks.org*
Code: IO035

Topic: Precipitation
Go to: *www.scilinks.org*
Code: IO036

with the proper supervision and planning. A wealth of resources exists on the subject of field study; the common theme in these resources is providing the opportunity for discovery in a local environment, whether it be a park stream, school campus, or coastal tide pool.

A Content Primer

After gaining some understanding of water quality analysis and the role of key elements in an ecosystem, we are ready to move on to the study of living organisms within the terrestrial and aquatic ecosystems, focusing mainly on forest and stream habitats. These two foci connect to the themes of mapping and water quality analysis in an integral manner and will later connect to the field and laboratory activities presented in previous chapters.

Definition of Biodiversity

Biodiversity can be defined as the variation of taxonomic life forms within a given ecosystem or biome, or for the entire Earth. A wide variety of organisms found in an ecosystem on a consistent basis can indicate "high" biodiversity, while a large number of only a few types can indicate "low" biodiversity. Biodiversity can be used as a

measure of the health of an ecosystem, to indicate what has existed from past to present, and to use native populations as a barometer for detecting introduced or invasive species.

Biodiversity can be determined in a similar manner in both terrestrial and aquatic ecosystems and serves the same importance in maintaining ecosystem stability. There are numerous methods for observing and analyzing biodiversity. These methods include both qualitative measures, which focus on what is observed and the described characteristics, and intricately quantitative analyses with sophisticated calculations. In this chapter we will keep the background and methods of measuring biodiversity on a fundamental level while providing an introduction to basic quantitative measures for practical fieldwork.

Determinants of Biodiversity

Precipitation and temperature are the primary determinants of biodiversity and are directly related to the latitude and/or geographic location of the ecosystem. For example, because of the greater average annual rainfall along with year-round warmer temperatures, biodiversity is larger in a tropical rain forest compared with a temperate deciduous one. As one approaches the poles, biodiversity decreases overall. In between these locations there is wide variation, but the overall trend is the same. This general relationship between latitude and biodiversity is represented in Figure 6.2.

Plant life also plays a significant role in the biodiversity story by creating habitats and encouraging the full potential of biodiversity in a specific ecosystem. From terrestrial temperate forests to marine kelp forests (see Figure 6.3), plants maintain the stability of an ecosystem and have established relationships with native species

FIGURE 6.2
Relationship Between Latitude and Biodiversity

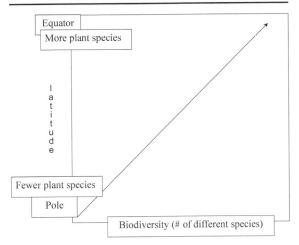

FIGURE 6.3
Kelp

from bacteria to animal life. Such relationships can also be illustrated on your school grounds by the establishment of native plant and wildflower gardens or other habitats that not only increase plant biodiversity but also attract a variety of organisms (see, e.g., the orb weaver spider in Figure 6.4).

FIGURE 6.4
Orb Weaver Spider

How Do We Measure Biodiversity?

Qualitative measures of biodiversity include writing descriptions of species that are found, drawing pictures, using photographs to document species, and using journals to keep notes about species. These observations can be extended to include calculations based on the probability of finding a species in a given area that is sampled.

Quantitative measurements include counting the total number of organisms as well as the total number of different species found within a study site. For example, Table 6.1 (p. 114) shows that the total number of spiders found within a study site was 100, and of this total number only three different species were represented. If you choose you can stop there and have students make simple inferences from the numbers and types of spiders present (e.g., whether one type of spider is found more frequently, or what type of location each is found in). Or students can use these data to perform biodiversity calculations.

TABLE 6.1
Sample Biodiversity Measurement

Kinds of Spider Found	Number of Each Kind of Spider
Garden spider	30
Crab spider	5
Jumping spider	65
Total number of spiders	100
Total number of species	3

FIGURE 6.5
Crab Spider

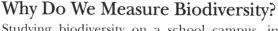

Topic: Maintaining Biodiversity

Go to: www.scilinks.org

Code: IO038

Of importance for this next step in quantitative biodiversity assessment is the value of the total number of species, *species richness* (*S*), as well as the fraction (probability expressed as a percentage) of each species relative to the whole. For example, the value for species richness in Table 6.1 is $S = 3$. As modeled in Table 6.2, finding the percentage of each species is a simple calculation. This percentage can then be discussed in terms of the *probability* of finding a particular species within a study site. Using these data students can say, for example, that the probability of finding a crab spider (Figure 6.5) is 5%.

Why Do We Measure Biodiversity?

Studying biodiversity on a school campus, in a forest ecosystem, or in an aquatic ecosystem requires some basic understanding of general trends in biodiversity due to factors such as geography, abiotic conditions, and plant life. Using biodiversity measurements with students can be a fun and engaging process and should take advantage of school grounds or other environmental sites that will give students the opportunity to observe their local environment and develop a better sense of local flora and fauna that can be carried back to the classroom.

TABLE 6.2
Sample Biodiversity Data and Calculations of Species Richness (*S*) and Probability (%)

Species Richness (*S* = 3)	Number Found	Equation	Result (%)
Garden spider	30	$30/100 = 0.30 \times 100$	30
Crab spider	5	$5/100 = 0.05 \times 100$	5
Jumping spider	65	$65/100 = 0.65 \times 100$	65
Total number	100		

Biodiversity Activities

Simply looking at organisms that inhabit a local environment and recording their presence is a basic start to any biodiversity study. Here, we will illustrate simple methods to assess biodiversity in and around your schoolyard in the hope that questions raised by such observations can provide the foundation for schoolyard action projects such as those discussed in Chapter 7. Plants provide the simplest observation mainly because they are immobile and easy to see. If you move into the realm of mobile organisms, there are excellent resources for observing birds, butterflies, and spiders. A simple writing log can be used to record where and when a species (if it can be identified) was found. Such detailed observations can be useful later on, especially in schoolyard habitat projects.

The easiest way to perform a quantitative estimate of biodiversity of the local habitat is to conduct sampling activities that will help "capture" organisms to be observed. The term *capture* can be interpreted literally, or it can mean to sample a snapshot of a particular local environment. Following are activities that allow for both qualitative and quantitative skills.

Activity 1. Leaf Litter Fun

An excellent site for a habitat inquiry is one with leaf litter (Figure 6.6). A pile of fallen leaves can be found just about anywhere around a schoolyard. Leaf litter samples can supply a bounty of organisms, from ants (insects) to spiders and other arachnids. Collecting is simple—just scoop up some leaf litter, place it in a plastic

FIGURE 6.6
Sample of Leaf Litter

A sample of leaf litter ready to be placed into a Berlese funnel. Some common inhabitants of leaf litter include (from left to right) a spider, a sow bug, and a millipede, as seen through the lens of a dissecting microscope (10×).

container, and take it back to the classroom. There are a number of variations on what to do next, but this activity includes some common elements that will help you along. You can also adapt the Soil Test Kit Results Data Sheet from Chapter 4, Activity 4 (p. 82), to fit data collection for leaf litter.

Driving Question

How can we estimate the biodiversity of a local habitat?

Materials

(We are collecting live samples so no preservative is used in the bottom of bottle.)

- Shallow trays—white is best because the "creepy crawlies" are easier to see (plastic ice cube trays found at any discount store work well)

- Trowel or small scoop to collect sample

- Simple lamps or light sources with 40–60 W bulb (ideally one per student group) (Caution: Hot bulbs can burn skin.)

- Empty 2-liter soda bottle or plastic funnel

- Plastic or glass jar

- Window screen (available at home improvement stores)

- Tape (masking tape works well)

- Dissecting microscope and/or magnifying glass (available from any science education supplier)

- Plastic ziplock bags

- Permanent marker for labeling (use low- or non-VOC marker)

- Petri dish (available from any science education supplier)

- Data sheet

Procedure

Provide students with the following instructions:

1. Obtain a leaf litter sample from a natural area or schoolyard. Scoop the litter and debris to the soil surface, but do not dig into the soil. Collect enough to fill a plastic sandwich bag, and label with date and source location.

2. A Berlese funnel can be used to separate the living organisms from the leaves (see Figure 6.7). Cut off the top 5 inches of the 2-liter soda bottle to make a "funnel." Tape a piece of screen over the bottle opening. Invert the funnel into the bottom portion of the soda bottle.

3. Tape the funnel to the bottom portion of the soda bottle to hold it in place temporarily. (If this is not done, the funnel will slide completely into the bottle.)

Activity 1 Data Sheet

Item Name	Quantity	Description (body parts, legs, etc.)

FIGURE 6.7
A Berlese Funnel Can Easily Be Made From a 2-Liter Soda Bottle.

magnifying glass. Some fine debris will be mixed with the organisms, so you will need to poke around. After scanning the sample, try to identify some of the main types of species, such as spiders, mites, worms, beetles, and various types of larvae. Record the species on the data sheet. Use the website BugGuide. net (*http://bugguide.net/node/view/15740*) as a reference for identification. Wash hands with soap and water.

Think About

1. Which organisms were the most numerous? Why do you think so?

2. What relationship is there between the time of year of your collection of leaf litter and the types and numbers of organisms found?

3. How else might you use a Berlese funnel for a biodiversity study?

Activity 2. Analysis of Plant and Animal Habitat in a Square Meter[1]

Driving Question

How can we estimate plant and animal biodiversity in a square meter plot or other predetermined lot of land?

Materials
(per group of three to four students)

- For a square meter plot, use four 1-meter, ½-inch PVC tubes with four right-angle elbows to make a square (available at home improvement stores). As an alternative use other predetermined shapes, such as a hula

4. Place the leaf litter sample into the prepared funnel.

5. Place a lamp with an incandescent lightbulb (40–60 W) near the top of the litter but not touching the sample, because the bulb will get hot.

6. Let the setup stand on a table (well ventilated), and observe organisms dropping from the funnel into the bottom of the soda bottle.

7. Transfer the organisms into a petri dish and examine under a dissecting microscope or

---

[1]   This activity is derived from the classic "Life in a Square Meter" from R. Gardner, S. Tocci, and P. J. Perry, *Ace Your Ecology and Environmental Science Project: Great Science Fair Ideas* (Berkeley Heights; NJ: Enslow Publishers, 2009).

1 meter x 1 meter
study plot

Square meter diagram

hoop, a wooden ring, a needlepoint ring, or some other object that is appropriate for a specific study site.

- Circle cutout (transparency sheets can be used for easy viewing, but you can also use plastic plate cutouts, coat hangers bent in a circle, or anything else that allows students to attain a sample of the whole)

- Blank Square Meter Diagram and data sheets for recording items found (use Activity 1 Data Sheet (p. 116) as a model)

- Metric ruler and/or tape measure

- Magnifying glass and/or hand lens

- Compass (available from science education suppliers and outdoor recreation stores)

Procedure

Give students the following instructions:

1. With your partner, use a compass to determine the directions of north, east, south, and west within your square meter. Indicate these directions by drawing a compass rose on your Square Meter Diagram (see Figure 6.8 as an example).

2. The area you analyze is to be chosen at random, so toss the cutout circle into the square meter, hula hoop, or other predetermined area. Make your observations within the circle. *Do not move the circle.* Indicate the placement of the circle by drawing and labeling it "Sample #1" on your Square Meter Diagram (see Figure 6.8).

3. Identify items (plants and animals) in the sample, and name each item. (NOTE TO TEACHER: The name can be any descriptor the students use—the name does not have to be the exact name for the item.)

4. Count how many of each item are found in the sample circle. An example of a teacher illustration is shown in Figure 6.9.

5. Describe the items (plants and animals) found in the sample, and include the descriptions (size, color, shape, texture) on the data sheet. For example, a student might describe a plant as "12 cm tall, 18 cm wide, with yellow flower and jagged, fuzzy, green leaves at the base."

6. Select another area as in step 2 and label it "Sample #2." Repeat steps 3–5 for this sample. Use additional data sheets for additional sample sites.

Think About

1. In what ways are sample areas different and the same?

2. What might be reasons for having more of one type of plant or animal versus another?

3. How might you refine this study to improve the accuracy of your data?

FIGURE 6.8
Sample Square Meter Diagram

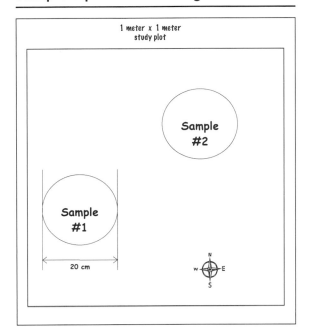

FIGURE 6.9
A Teacher Illustration of a Plant Biodiversity Activity

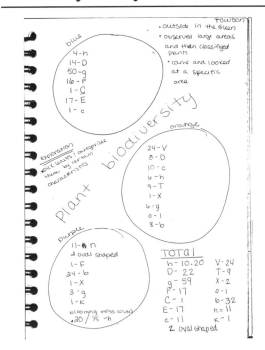

Activity 3.
Macroinvertebrate Analysis

Sampling of aquatic macroinvertebrates is one part of the whole picture of water quality analysis of a stream. A number of environmental organizations, including the Chesapeake Bay Foundation (*www.cbf.org/Page.aspx?pid=260*) and Virginia Save Our Streams (*www.vasos.org/pages/downloads.html*), provide computational methods using macroinvertebrate data to determine a more precise measure of stream quality.

The method for organism collection varies, but the basic premise is to locate a fairly fast-moving stream, one that is moving over rocks in very shallow water (referred to as riffles; see Chapter 2). In this activity you and your students will use a standard kick net and other basic equipment to collect as many organisms as possible, and then identify, count, and categorize these organisms.

Along with assessing biodiversity of macroinvertebrates we recommend that students complete chemical tests of the stream. We do this to obtain a complete picture of the health of a particular stream site. When taken separately both chemical and biological indicators are important components in assessing stream health, but the combination of abiotic and biotic factors gives a much clearer picture of stream quality. For example, chemical analysis is only a momentary "snapshot" of the stream chemistry at that time. While useful to detect recent chemical and nutrient loading, this analysis is somewhat limited in its predictive ability. Biological sampling offers information relative to the long-term health of a stream and is useful for a more global assessment of stream quality. Most sampled organisms are sedentary, not moving rapidly or far, and thus their presence or absence gives a better enduring indication of stream quality.

Driving Questions

1. How can we determine habitat quality of a stream?

2. What can macroinvertebrate diversity tell us about stream health?

Materials

- Shallow trays—white is best because the "creepy crawlies" are easier to see (plastic ice cube trays found at any discount store work well)

- Soft brushes (kitchen brushes work well and are available at home supply or grocery stores)

- Buckets

- Magnifying glass

- Kick net (available from biological education suppliers—we suggest the LaMotte Company Student Grade Kick Net available at *www.lamotte.com*)

- Hand net (available at pet or aquarium stores)

- Laminated macroinvertebrate identification charts (see Figure 6.10)

- Laminated data sheets

Procedure
Part I. Collection

1. Locate a riffle to study.

2. Have students place the kick net in the water at the sample site. The bottom of the net should face upstream, and the top should be tilted downstream (see Figure 6.11, p. 123).

3. Using their feet, students should "shuffle" the rocks and cobbles above the net to dislodge organisms so that they "flow" into the net.

4. Have students "wash" organisms (using water from a bucket) into a sample container.

5. Have students pick up any movable stones and cobbles and gently brush them over the bucket to dislodge any additional organisms.

Part II. Counting and Categorizing

The Maryland Department of Natural Resources (DNR) lists three major categories of macro-invertebrates (you can print out and laminate the identification sheet from *www.dnr.state.md.us/streams/pubs/dnr_bugsheet.pdf*; see Figure 6.10):

- Sensitive Organisms (sensitive to pollution; typically found in healthy streams)

- Moderately-Sensitive Organisms (moderately sensitive to pollution; found in healthy or fair-quality streams)

- Tolerant Organisms (tolerant to pollution; found in healthy, fair-quality, or poor-quality streams)

1. Using the Maryland DNR identification sheet determine

   a. the total number of organisms found,

   b. the species richness (S) of the sample, and

   c. the total number of organisms in each category (sensitive, moderately sensitive, and tolerant).

2. Use these data to make calculations about stream quality (see Table 6.3, p. 123).

FIGURE 6.10
Stream Macroinvertebrates

Stream Macroinvertebrates
Maryland Department of Natural Resources

C. Ronald Franks, Secretary

Robert L. Ehrlich Jr., Governor

Relative abundances in Maryland are indicated by "rare", "common", or "abundant". The number of families in Maryland for higher taxonomic levels are also listed (if applicable). Sizes are for "full grown" animals. To learn more about these fascinating creatures, go to http://www.dnr.maryland.gov/bay/cblife/insects/index.html. To learn about DNR's volunteer stream monitoring program, Maryland Stream Waders, send an inquiry to streamwaders@dnr.state.md.us.

SENSITIVE ORGANISMS
POLLUTION-SENSITIVE ORGANISMS TYPICALLY FOUND IN HEALTHY STREAMS

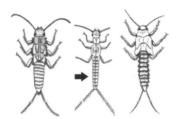

Mayfly: Order Ephemeroptera- Plate-like or feathery gills on sides of lower body (arrow); three (sometimes 2) long, hair-like tails; 1"; abundant; 11 families.

Stonefly: Order Plecoptera- Two hair-like tails; six jointed legs with two hooked tips each; big antennae; no gills on lower half of body (arrow); 1⅜"; abundant: 9 families.

Caddisfly: Order Trichoptera- Six jointed, hooked legs just behind head; 2 hooks at back end; may be in a case made of stones, leaves or sticks; non-netspinning caddisflies have no bushy gills along bottom; 1"; abundant; 20 families.

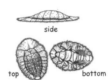

side

top   bottom

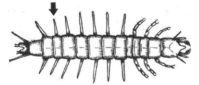

Water Penny: Order Coleoptera- shaped like a tiny, grey, oblong frisbee; 6 tiny legs on bottom; slow crawler; ¼"; common.

Hellgrammite and Fishfly: Order Megaloptera- dark body; six jointed legs; large, pinching jaws; many pointed feelers along edge of body (arrow); two small hooks at back end; hellgrammites have feathery tufts of gills along side of body; 4"; rare.

Gilled Snail: Class Gastropoda- shell opens on the right and is covered by a hard shield-like operculum; 1"; rare; 4 families.

MODERATELY-SENSITIVE ORGANISMS
MODERATELY POLLUTION-SENSITIVE ORGANISMS FOUND IN HEALTHY OR FAIR QUALITY STREAMS

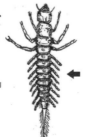

Net-spinning Caddisfly: Order Trichoptera- six jointed, hooked legs just behind head; 2 hooks at back end; bushy gills along lower half (arrow); 1"; abundant.

Alderfly: Order Megaloptera- six jointed legs; pinching jaws; many pointed feelers along edge of body (arrow); long tail at the end; 1"; rare.

Crane Fly: Order Diptera- worm-like; no jointed legs; head hidden inside the light brown body; 4 finger-like lobes at back end (arrow); 2"; abundant.

FIGURE 6.10 (*continued*)
Stream Macroinvertebrates

MODERATELY-SENSITIVE ORGANISMS (continued)

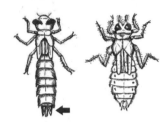

Dragonfly: Order Odonata- large eyes; bullet-shaped, round or leaf-like body; 6 long legs; 3 short-spike-like tails (arrow); may have wing pads; 2"; common; 6 families.

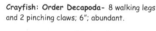

Damselfly: Order Odonata- 6 long, thin legs; 3 broad oval tails at end (arrow); may have wing pads; no gills along sides of body; 2"; common; 3 families.

adult

larva

Riffle Beetle: Order Coleoptera - 6 jointed legs; brown or black; adults have hard covering over the wings, body with fairly hard covering; 3/8"; abundant.

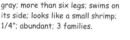

Scud: Order Amphipoda - white to gray; more than six legs; swims on its side; looks like a small shrimp; 1/4"; abundant; 3 families.

Clams and mussels: Class Bivalvia - two hinged hard shells; 5"; rare; 2 families.

Crayfish: Order Decapoda- 8 walking legs and 2 pinching claws; 6"; abundant.

TOLERANT ORGANISMS
POLLUTION-TOLERANT ORGANISMS FOUND IN HEALTHY, FAIR OR POOR QUALITY STREAMS

Non-biting Midge: Order Diptera - dark head; body white, gray or reddish; worm-like segmented body; 2 tiny unjointed legs on both ends (arrow); ½"; abundant.

Black Fly: Order Diptera - shaped like a little bowling pin; black head with tiny bristles for filtering food (arrow); suction pad on end; no jointed legs; ½"; abundant.

Leech: Order Hirudinea - brown or grey, slimy, suction pads on both ends (arrow); 2"; rare; 3 families.

Ramshorn Snails: Class Gastropoda - No hard cover over opening; shell coiled in one plane; ½"; common.

Aquatic worm: Class Oligochaeta - thin and hairlike or thicker like an earthworm; 2 ½"; common; 8

Pouch Snail: Class Gastropoda - shell opens on the left; no hard covering over shell opening; 3/4"; common.

 Maryland Department of Natural Resources; Resource Assessment Service; 580 Taylor Avenue; Annaoplis, Maryland 21401
www.dnr.maryland.gov; toll free in MD 1-877-620-8DNR (dial 9 then extension 8623)
TTY users call via MD Relay

Published March 2004

Source: Maryland Department of Natural Resources: Resource Assessment Service, *www.dnr.maryland.gov.*

Think About

1. How can the numbers of organisms in each category be used to determine the health of a stream?

2. Why do we combine chemical water analysis and biodiversity assessment of a stream when determining the water quality of that site?

Activity 4. Biofilms and Biodiversity

Introducing methods to teachers that are simple, are inexpensive, and provide excellent avenues for student inquiry and exploration is essential, especially at the elementary level. A method for studying aquatic life that does not require nets, seines, or boots can be a budgetary relief and reduce preparation time on the part of the teacher and student group. The methods adapted here have been used for years all over the world, but their practical methodology has had little exposure in the K–12 classroom.

In 1997, Maryland Sea Grant launched a web page titled "Biofilms and Biodiversity" (*www.mdsg.umd.edu/programs/education/interactive_lessons/biofilm/index.htm*) that came from research being performed at the Center of Marine Biotechnology in the laboratory of Dr. William R. Jones and his research associate Mike Ewell, who was studying the settling rate of oyster larvae on inverted glass petri dish lids held in a wooden

FIGURE 6.11
Using a Kick Net

Dr. Robert Blake and Towson University preservice elementary education students use a kick net in a stream on campus.

rack. The community of organisms that grew on the lids, and associated visitors, provided a unique window into the world of aquatic organisms through the microscope (see, e.g., Figure 6.12, p. 124).

TABLE 6.3
Sample Data Categorized by Organism Sensitivity to Pollution

Organism Sensitivity Category (S = 3)	Number Found	Equation to Determine % of Each in Sample	%
Sensitive	60	60/100 = 0.60 × 100	60
Moderately sensitive	25	25/100 = 0.25 × 100	25
Tolerant	15	15/100 = 0.15 × 100	15

FIGURE 6.12
Dusky Sea Slug

The rack system has since had many design modifications to simplify it; its present composition is inexpensive PVC pipe and discs made from acrylic, blank CDs, or any other substrate to be tested for its habitability (Frederick, Jacobs, and Jones 2000). In the field of science similar sampling devices are known as Hester-Dendy plates (a ceramic material) and can be found in many environmental science catalogs for approximately $25–$30. However, if a transparent material (acrylic) is used, then a whole new world of options opens up for microscopic examination of the intact community—where the real excitement lies for teachers and students.

Materials and Procedure for a Biofilms and Biodiversity Exploration

The method for constructing a biodiversity rack system is outlined on the Maryland Sea Grant website and is illustrated in Figures 6.13 and 6.14.

Observing biofilm communities follows a progression to develop an improved visual picture of what is being observed:

1. You begin with the naked eye.

FIGURE 6.13
Biodiversity Rack Design

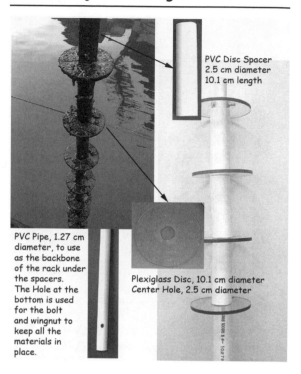

PVC Disc Spacer 2.5 cm diameter 10.1 cm length

PVC Pipe, 1.27 cm diameter, to use as the backbone of the rack under the spacers. The Hole at the bottom is used for the bolt and wingnut to keep all the materials in place.

Plexiglass Disc, 10.1 cm diameter Center Hole, 2.5 cm diameter

FIGURE 6.14
Biodiversity Racks

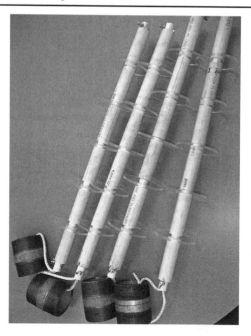

2. You progress to magnifying glass (see Figure 6.15).

3. You then progress to a dissecting microscope (low power—up to 45×).

Developing this progression of observation is important because teachers may have an untrained eye with regard to microscopy. For example, in Figure 6.15 the visible community of living things can be observed with the naked eye and magnifying glass, but at this point most may describe it simply as "slime." However, at the microscopic level more specific organisms are seen (Figure 6.16).

At this stage for both teacher and students the primary importance is not to identify the exact species of organism but to see that a variety of organisms exist and to eventually determine what types they are (phylum and/or class).

Wrap-Up

Biodiversity measures are often the benchmark used in determining the overall quality and health of an ecosystem (or even a habitat). In the discussion of habitat restoration, some scientists believe that it will be necessary to restore entire biomes (e.g., the Great Plains in the central United States) on a large scale for sustained conservation and restoration of degraded ecosystems (see information from the 3rd National Conference on Ecosystem Restoration, *http://conference.ifas.ufl.edu/NCER2009*). However, such grand visions should not prevent us from encouraging students to begin this process locally. Thus, biodiversity studies are an excellent means to initiate habitat assessments and lead directly into student construction of action projects.

FIGURE 6.15
View of a Biofilm Community With a Magnifying Glass

Topic: Changes in Ecosystems

Go to: *www.scilinks.org*

Code: I0039

FIGURE 6.16
Microscopic View of a Biofilm Community Showing Bryozoans

Resource List
Printed Material

Frederick, J. A., D. Jacobs, and W. R. Jones. 2000. Biofilms and biodiversity: An interactive exploration of aquatic microbial biotechnology and ecology. *Journal of*

Industrial Microbiology and Biotechnology 24 (55): 334–338.

Gardner, R., S. Tocci, and P. J. Perry. 2009. *Ace your ecology and environmental science project: Great science fair ideas.* Berkeley Heights, NJ: Enslow Publishers.

Websites

Bug identification guide
 http://bugguide.net/node/view/15740
Chesapeake Bay Foundation
 http://www.cbf.org/Page.aspx?pid=260

Maryland Department of Natural Resources ("Stream Macro-invertebrates")
 www.dnr.state.md.us/streams/pubs/dnr_bugsheet.pdf
Maryland Sea Grant
 www.mdsg.umd.edu/programs/education/interactive_lessons/biofilm/index.htm
3rd National Conference on Ecosystem Restoration
 http://conference.ifas.ufl.edu/NCER2009
Virginia Save Our Streams
 www.vasos.org/pages/downloads.html

7

Action Projects

A Content Primer
Why Action Projects?

In previous chapters we presented fundamental science content embedded within environmental science and showcased numerous activities you can use to engage students in outdoor learning. Although each chapter represents this content individually, as separate pieces of a puzzle, we want teachers and students to learn these concepts in an integrated manner by using outdoor action projects to increase understanding. While *knowing* content of the science disciplines is important, effective environmentally based curricula must go beyond this aspect and have an impact on students' way of *thinking* as well as their *behavior*. Most environmental educators agree that a sound environmental program should achieve three goals:

1. increase student science content knowledge,

2. effect a positive change of student attitude toward the environment, and

3. effect a positive change of student behavior in regard to the environment.

Simply put, an increase in the content knowledge of environmental science leads to a better understanding of an environmental issue. This understanding leads to a change in attitude, which then brings about a positive change in behavior. Although changes in attitude and behavior are more difficult to measure and also more difficult to achieve than increased understanding, our intent is to create young citizens who are well informed on the environmental issues affecting their communities and willing to take action to address these issues.

In this chapter we offer suggestions on how to plan action projects with your students that address environmental issues of importance, whether in your school grounds or in your community. We offer suggestions of how to begin this process, where to seek partnerships and funding, and how to garner support from faculty, administrators, and parents. Finally, we showcase actual student projects, including a storm drain rain garden, a native plant garden, habitat restoration, and a schoolwide focus on saving the local watershed.

How to Choose an Action Project

The best action projects are ones that serve to address a local environmental issue in the schoolyard or in the community and can be easily integrated into the existing science curriculum. Without a preexisting topic to study, the simplest way to begin is to complete the Schoolyard Report Card from Chapter 2. Using this assessment, students collect data pertaining to the schoolyard and then determine where improvements can be made. For example, if erosion seems to be a concern, students may elect to construct a rain garden or native plant garden that will absorb runoff after rainstorms. If there is a lack of habitat or food supply for animals, students may choose to plant native species that

will provide fruit, nuts, or other food sources. A lack of habitat can also be addressed by adding such structures as bat boxes, bluebird nest boxes, toad houses, and rock gardens. With these myriad of possibilities the important point to remember is to have students use an assessment to determine need. The schoolyard assessment also serves the dual function of providing students with the ability to analyze data and play a role in choosing the project.

Integrating Action Projects Into Subject Area Content

We have found that the most common reason teachers give for choosing not to involve students in environmental action projects is that there is neither time nor resources to fit anything extra into an already overfilled curriculum, and many teachers tend to see these projects as an "add-on." However, if the environmental concepts to be taught and the projects chosen are closely aligned with state and national curricular standards, then teachers need to only teach the curriculum using an environmental approach rather than teaching the curriculum inside the classroom, in a traditional setting. These environmental concepts also have value for integration into other disciplines, thus there are a variety of ways to engage students in these types of experiences.

For example, let's assume that Mrs. Jones, a fourth-grade teacher, has a unit in her science curriculum that covers the concept of life cycles. For the past five years, she has taught the unit using butterfly larvae purchased from a biological supply company. The larvae are housed in the classroom until they hatch. The children observe them daily and record their observations in their science journals. This year, Mrs. Jones decides to have her students plan a butterfly garden plot on the school grounds. The students research the types of plants needed to attract both adult and larval stages of the butterflies, determine how many plants will fit into the designated space, write letters to local community nurseries asking for donations, and finally procure the plants and create their garden. The plants are on the school grounds for many years to come, and each year Mrs. Jones takes her students outside to the butterfly garden to observe the various life stages they have learned about in class.

Science is not the only subject that can be integrated into an environmental action project. Listed below are some ways we have seen classroom teachers integrate various subject areas in their own projects.

- *Mathematics:* measuring the area of a garden plot, calculating the total cost of a project for grant applications, determining how many plants will fit into a single plot, measuring water temperature of a stream, measuring wood to cut in order to construct nest boxes

- *Language arts:* writing to persuade the school principal to allow an action project to be completed, writing to persuade a grantor to fund the project, writing to inform others why the project is important, visiting a completed action project site to write poetry or record observations, writing articles or letters to the editor to raise public awareness

- *Social studies:* incorporating politics and government into projects on environmental policy and local laws, writing to government officials regarding environmental issues in the community, studying the human impact on the environment and the history of land use near the school or in the community, creating a timeline of events

- *Art:* making habitat posters, public service brochures highlighting local environmental issues, fish print T-shirts, and handmade notepaper featuring local wildlife drawings

Garnering Support
School-Based Support

A successful environmental action project needs support from the school administration, faculty and staff, and parents. Before you start planning the project, make sure you have the necessary backing from relevant personnel at your school. Start with your administrator. Make sure he or she is aware of what you are planning, how it enhances learning experiences for your students, and how your plans are aligned with the curriculum. You will also want to obtain the support of your school grounds crew or custodial staff. We have unfortunately witnessed many "mow-overs" after projects were completed—incidents where the students created garden plots that were destroyed the next time the school grounds were mowed because the groundskeepers were not aware of the plantings. The groundskeepers may also assist with the care of the plants (such as watering needs) if they are made aware of what you and your class are planning.

Environmental action projects almost always come with a cost. The classroom teacher may be left wondering how to fund these projects. Here is a list of suggestions for funding, drawn from our experiences:

- Check with your school PTO/PTA. They may be willing to donate funds or assist with a fundraiser.

- Investigate parents as a resource. Do any of them own a landscaping business, nursery, or mulch business? Can any of them donate or lend lumber or tools? One school we worked with was able to obtain an entire truckload of mulch for free. Another was able to use gardening tools without having to purchase them. Still another obtained lumber for a nature trail free of cost. All of these items were obtained from parents.

Community-Based Support
Local

While having the support of the school members is essential to the success of your project, you will enhance the likelihood of success by partnering with community organizations as well. We have found that many organizations will contribute to your project if it fits into their mission and goals. Local colleges and universities may also be willing to offer expertise in the science content and may have resources for funding. (As university faculty, we have assisted many schools in completing action projects.) Cooperative extension agencies (often affiliated with colleges and universities) may also be able to assist you with technical issues related to your project site, such as determining soil type and even soil testing.

If asked, local businesses will often donate or discount materials needed to complete the project. For example, we were once given 1,000 pounds of rock for a school rock garden from the local rock quarry. In addition, a cooperating teacher contacted a local nursery and, upon informing the clerk that she was purchasing for a school, was given the wholesale price instead of retail.

Regional/National

There are many national environmental education programs that can serve as a resource for field-based learning. For example, Project Learning Tree (PLT), which is sponsored by the American Forest Foundation, includes action components in many of the activities published in the preK–8 curriculum guide, as well as the secondary modules designed for grades 9–12.

PLT also sponsors *GreenWorks!*, a service learning/community action program that partners PLT educators, students, and community in environmental neighborhood improvement projects. *GreenWorks!* blends service activities with the academic curriculum and addresses real community needs as students learn through active engagement. Some examples of past grant projects include habitat restoration, watershed improvement, outdoor classrooms, and energy conservation.

Several states across the country have implemented Green Schools programs, programs that recognize schools that commit to environmentally friendly practices, both in the curricula and in the completion of field-based action projects. One of the oldest and most successful is the state of Maryland's Green Schools program, which began in 1998 and, to date, has certified almost 300 schools across the state. The goal of all these programs is to get students involved in making changes in their school environments and local communities that result in greater environmental awareness and healthier environments for all.

Another option to consider is writing a grant. Many agencies that award funds for action projects have grant applications that are very teacher and student friendly and actually require student involvement in the grant-writing process (*GreenWorks!* and the Chesapeake Bay Trust, to name just two).

Process and Completion of the Project

Once you decide on a project, the next step is implementation. On the day of your culminating activity, make sure that you are well organized. Each student should have something to do, and there should be enough adults present to properly supervise them. Ask for parent volunteers or, better yet, representatives from those agencies and businesses that donated funding or supplies for your project to help you supervise. Consider safety issues that may need addressing and review any precautions with your students and the adults who are supervising them. If the site of your action project is not on school grounds, you will need to arrange for transportation to and from the site. Some key reminders and tips from teachers who have gone through this process are included later in this chapter.

In this section we present examples of action projects completed at actual schools. First, we will describe a single classroom–based project that focused on runoff prevention by planting a native plant garden around a storm drain. Second, we will describe a schoolwide project involving the construction of a native plant garden. The third example is a schoolwide project involving multiple grade levels, a project best summarized as a wetlands restoration venture with students' removing invasive plants and replacing them with native ones. Finally, we will describe another project involving multiple grade levels, focused on saving the local watershed.

Single Classroom–Based Project: A Storm Drain Rain Garden

The lead teacher at this school was a participant in a grant project awarded from the National Oceanic and Atmospheric Administration (NOAA). Participants completed a weeklong summer workshop focusing on local watershed issues and how to address those issues with elementary-level children. Each participant was required to carry out an action project with their students. After investigating the school grounds and completing the Schoolyard Report Card, the students (grade 4) decided that their schoolyard was suffering from issues related to *lack of native plant species, runoff,* and *erosion*. The chosen action project was a rain garden filled with native plants. The purpose of the rain garden was to absorb rainwater before it ran off onto

FIGURE 7.1
Storm Drain Rain Garden Before Planting

FIGURE 7.2
Storm Drain Rain Garden After Planting

impervious surfaces on school grounds, thus alleviating problems resulting from erosion or pollutants that may be carried by the rainwater.

Rain gardens are a common choice for action projects; they can fit into almost any schoolyard and are often combined with a native plant garden. Potential locations for rain gardens are simple to identify. Any area near a storm drain, an area that has standing water after a storm, or even an area that remains wet longer than the surrounding landscape is a good choice for a rain garden (see Figures 7.1 and 7.2). In fact, rain gardens are such a common action project that an internet search reveals a number of websites that show teachers and students how to construct one (Table 7.1).

Schoolwide Single Project: A Native Plant Garden

Whether associated with a storm drain or as a stand-alone site, a native plant garden is an excellent project for students at all grade levels. Again, to determine a suitable site students can use the Schoolyard Report Card from Chapter 2. For example, students may choose an area of continuous standing water and plant wetland, or moisture-tolerant plants. Or, if the goal is habitat restoration, specifically to attract native insects,

TABLE 7.1
Sample of Internet Resources for Rain Gardens

Government Agencies	
U.S. Environmental Protection Agency	*www.epa.gov/waste/conserve/rrr/greenscapes/owners.htm* or search for "rain gardens" at *www.epa.gov*
Illinois Sustainable Infrastructure Initiative	*http://raingarden.il.gov*
Maine Department of Environmental Protection	*www.maine.gov/tools/whatsnew/index.php?topic=IOB&id=4713&v=Article*
Maryland Department of Natural Resources	*www.dnr.state.md.us/ed/editorials/RainGarden-Final.pdf*
Wisconsin Department of Natural Resources	*www.dnr.state.wi.us/runoff/rg*
Institutions of Higher Education	
Alabama Cooperative Extension System	*www.aces.edu/waterquality/nemo/Fact%20Sheets/rain%20garden,%20mg,%20final.pdf*
University of Delaware Cooperative Extension	*http://ag.udel.edu/extension/horticulture/raingarden*
University of Rhode Island Healthy Landscapes	*www.uri.edu/ce/healthylandscapes/raingarden.htm*
Conservation Organizations	
Chesapeake Bay Foundation	*www.cbf.org/Page.aspx?pid=1000*
Rain Garden Network	*www.raingardennetwork.com*

then a simple native plant and flower garden will suit this purpose (see Figure 7.3). To find native plants one need only go to the local nursery or, as in Maryland, consult an organization that specifically grows and sells native plants. For example, Environmental Concern's nursery website (*www.wetland.org/nursery_home.htm*) lists many plant species native to Maryland and the northeast United States. Native plants are the best choice for these projects because they also provide food and habitat for local animals.

Schoolwide Single Project: Habitat Restoration

As with the storm drain runoff project, the lead teachers for this project were also participants

FIGURE 7.3
Native Plant Garden

in the NOAA grant. Here, the students and teachers chose a marsh restoration as their action project. Similar to the rain garden construction, wetland restoration is a multistep process, and the first step is to identify a site for the action project. In this instance the site was identified in the fall (Figure 7.4). Students then assessed which plants were native and should be kept and which ones were invasive and should be removed. The plant removal was a multiclass endeavor conducted during the spring of the following year (Figure 7.5).

After plant removal and site preparation the teachers and students decided which plants to introduce back into the environment. At this step teachers can request help

from local and state groups, which is often an excellent means to promote school and community outreach connections. In this example the school contacted Environmental Concern (*www.wetland.org*) to purchase native plants to include in the project, which they first laid out to determine a planting pattern (Figure 7.6).

FIGURE 7.4
Marsh Restoration Site in the Fall

FIGURE 7.6
Marsh Restoration Site Planting Pattern

Every teacher was expected to integrate the action project into the curriculum they were normally expected to teach. Teachers were encouraged to integrate as many subject areas as possible into the project components, with language arts being a common subject area; students would write to their classroom teacher explaining what they learned from the action project.

The project was very popular in the community and a story about it appeared on the front page of the local newspaper the day after it was completed.

A year later we visited the site to assess the impact the restoration had. Figures 7.7 and 7.8 show the impressive growth of the new plants and how successful the project was.

FIGURE 7.5
Students at Marsh Restoration Site in the Spring

FIGURE 7.7
Marsh Restoration Site One Year Later

Schoolwide Multiple Projects

This final example is from a preK–8 private school in which the entire school undertook their activities as part of the requirements to meet the Maryland Green School certification. The schoolwide focus was simply to answer the question, How can we save our watershed? (In this case the watershed was the Chesapeake Bay.) Teachers in each grade level examined their curricula to determine an alignment between what they were required to teach and what they wanted to teach as it related to the watershed. The culminating action projects took place a few weeks before the end of the school year (2006), with each grade responsible for transforming part of the schoolyard. The following are examples of the projects:

- Planting trees to enhance the riparian buffer

- Planting a butterfly garden with native plants

- Designing a nature trail around the school to encourage students and faculty to investigate their surroundings

- Cleaning up a storm water pond and planting native wetland plants to encourage filtration of water and reduce runoff

FIGURE 7.8
Obedient Plant (*Physostegia virginiana*) at Marsh Restoration Site One Year Later

Each project was a part of a whole and shows how a school can embrace the simple concept of saving a watershed, leading to a schoolwide effort involving environmental action projects.

An Example of Changes in Attitude With Action Projects

We have emphasized the importance of instilling a sense of environmental stewardship in our students and, in so doing, bringing about a change in attitude and behavior as they relate to positive actions toward the environment. At one elementary school, students decided to build bluebird nest boxes to provide places for these birds to raise their young. These nest boxes have become increasingly important to bluebird survival as they have lost nesting sites in the wild and have also suffered from competition from non-native birds (in particular, European starlings). The classroom teacher working with these students administered surveys of student attitudes toward science to her students both before teaching any of the curricula related to the project and after the action project was completed. Although the sample size is small, the students in this class did demonstrate positive changes in attitude toward learning science and toward the environmental concepts they were taught.

Likewise, the teachers we worked with on these projects demonstrated a positive change in behavior and seemed more enthusiastic about taking their students outside in the future. The following is an excerpt from the journal kept by a teacher-participant throughout the project:

> *This has been a wonderful experience on both a personal and classroom level. I have always been interested in plants and gardening, so the NOAA program was right up my alley. However, the opportunity to explore the variety of habitats and plants exceeded my grandest dreams. In addition to the guest experts, I found other opportunities to extend my knowledge by speaking to professionals in the field. I attended a tree identification course at the National Zoo that enabled me to deliver information to the students who participated in the schoolyard habitat project. On the classroom level the project provided an invitation to stewardship. In addition to being the best fifth grade diggers in the county, my kids became truly interested and thoroughly involved in the planning, development, and future of the gardens they planted. They feel they have touched the future with their work and they feel gratified by their gesture. I feel that the schoolyard habitat project has been a worthy expenditure of time on both my part and the part of the students. It has allowed me to extend the soils, water, and wetlands program that county teachers use to an application level that is much more meaningful—it is a knowledge that will stick with the kids.*

Teacher Advice Regarding the Implementation of Action Projects

The words of advice listed in this section have been compiled from partner teachers based on their experiences completing an action project. We hope that the lessons gathered from these experiences can benefit teachers who are implementing projects for the first time.

- *What could be done in one day usually takes two days.* Every action project is different. Build in days that may or may not be used for planning, preparing, or planting.

- *Weathermen usually don't consider your project a top priority.* Build in rain dates on your action project days.

- *Never underestimate the willingness and ingenuity of your students.* Students often come up with the best ideas, and many are willing to volunteer their personal time and resources.

- *Remember the golden 20%.* Not all of your students will pour their heart and soul into your action project. However, there will always be about 20% of the students who will take ownership of the project.

- *Tactile learners are tenacious diggers, and bookworms are brilliant designers.* Some students do well in one part of your project, but not in other parts. As a teacher, be observant of the skills of your students. Reward them for their strengths, and encourage them in their weaknesses.

- *Catch your students doing something right.* When you are in the process of tedious tasks, like digging up soil, point out how well specific students are doing.

- *When in doubt, delegate.* There are certain parts of the project that you may not be comfortable with or have no knowledge of. When this happens, find someone who is comfortable and knowledgeable and ask them to help. This may mean involving parents, colleagues, or community members.

- *Think short and long term.* Have a general plan as to how to use the site of your action project over the next five years. Also, if your action project involves planting, think about who will take care of the area in the summer and in the future.

- *Warning! Teachable moment ahead!* There are many teachable moments involved in action projects. These moments can involve, for example, soil sampling, using math in scales and ratios, integrating art, using tools such as shovels, classifying organisms, introducing landscaping, practicing time management, and learning to make business phone calls or write business letters. One of the goals of doing a project is to empower students to create their own environmental action plan at home or in their communities.

- *Flexibility is important.* Nurseries can only carry so many plants. The plants that you have planned on may not be there, or there may not be as many as you have planned for, so you need to have a backup list of plants. Let your students know of this. Stay in contact with local nurseries regarding plant availability. If you need to order plants, make sure you give nurseries at least two months, especially in the winter months. The same applies to any other equipment you may need.

- *Is the juice worth the squeeze?* Yes, yes, yes! Having students participate in an action project can be one of the most rewarding aspects of the school year. There will be times when you will want to crawl into the hole your students just dug for a tree because you are so overwhelmed, but keep your chin up. These experiences will have a lasting impact on students that will endure much longer than many traditional classroom lessons. The end results and the praises your students will receive from other people are worth it!

- *Celebrate!* Your environmental action project may be months in the making, and your students and you will have contributed countless hours of planning and learning about the concepts behind the project by the project completion date. On the day your project is complete, you and your students are bound to feel a sense of pride in what you have accomplished. It is important to acknowledge your students for all their hard work and to celebrate their accomplishments (and yours). This celebration can be as large or as small as you wish it to be, but it is a very worthwhile thing to do. We have worked with schools that simply ended the day with a pizza party, and with schools that have had elaborate ceremonies complete with local and state government officials, superintendents, and news media crews. The most important thing it to let your students know that what they did matters and that you are proud of their efforts. When planning your celebration, consider inviting members of the community and parents so they can see for themselves what the students did. Your action project may end up serving as a model for others in the community to follow.

Wrap-Up

The action project is perhaps the most important piece within the entire framework of the "inside-out" concept. Action projects are an invaluable way to engage students in authentic, real-life application of the concepts they have learned relating to the environment and are a wonderful means of instilling a sense of environmental stewardship among students. In completing these projects students often gain a sense of pride in knowing that they can truly make a difference in the schoolyard or community environment.

Resource List
Websites

Alabama Master Gardens ("Rain Garden Design for Home Owners")
> *www.aces.edu/waterquality/nemo/Fact%20 Sheets/rain%20garden,%20mg,%20final.pdf*

Chesapeake Bay Foundation
> *www.cbf.org*

Chesapeake Bay Trust
> *www.cbtrust.org*

Environmental Concern
> *www.wetland.org; www.wetland.org/nursery_ home.htm* (nursery)

Illinois Sustainable Infrastructure Initiative
> *http://raingarden.il.gov*

Maine Department of Environmental Protection
> *www.maine.gov/tools/whatsnew/index. php?topic=IOB&id=4713&v=Article*

Maryland Department of Natural Resources, Environmental Design Program
> *www.dnr.state.md.us/ed/editorials/ RainGarden-Final.pdf*

National Oceanic and Atmospheric Administration
> *www.noaa.gov*

Project Learning Tree
> *www.plt.org*

Rain Garden Network
> *www.raingardennetwork.com*

University of Delaware Cooperative Extension
> *http://ag.udel.edu/extension/horticulture/ raingarden*

University of Rhode Island Healthy Landscapes
> *www.uri.edu/ce/healthylandscapes/raingarden. htm*

U.S. Environmental Protection Agency
> *www.epa.gov*

Wisconsin Department of Natural Resources
> *www.dnr.state.wi.us/runoff/rg*

8

Reflections on Implementation

We often hear from practicing teachers and especially preservice students that the ideas we have espoused in the previous chapters sound good in theory but are just not possible in the "real world" of the elementary and middle school classrooms. They comment that they do not have time, the materials, the content understanding, or even the confidence to engage students in field-based learning experiences. Circumstances seem so dire that when asked to reflect on the science teaching during their student teaching experience we have had preservice interns respond, "Science!? What science! We don't teach science."

In this chapter our intent is not to review the literature (as we did in the Introduction) that justifies and rationalizes the implementation of field-based learning experiences for elementary and middle school students and teachers. Our experience has been that if you find one principal or administrator or one or two teachers who have the interest, the passion, and a proactive attitude, a lot can be done with regard to field-based learning. We, therefore, provide here narrative statements on implementation from a variety of stakeholders in the process of environmental science education. Our hope is that reading these stories will inspire you to find ways to engage students in meaningful environmental science experiences and bring them "inside-out."

Christine Wolfe[1]: Creating a Schoolyard Habitat in Middle School

Wicomico Day School is a private, independent school on the lower eastern shore of Maryland.

---

[1] Christine Wolfe is a middle school computer science and mathematics teacher at Wicomico Day School, 1315 Old Ocean City Road, Salisbury, MD 21804; phone 410-546-5151.

Its mission is to provide a strong traditional education in a warm, friendly environment stressing family involvement. As a teacher at Wicomico Day School, I endeavored to enhance our curriculum with an environmental outdoor education program. A large part of that endeavor was the creation of a Schoolyard Habitat, a habitat restoration program developed by the National Wildlife Federation.

Often students find it difficult to relate to environmental concerns. They may not have been exposed to pollution from large cities or experience the effects of deforestation. It is important to educate students about their impact on the environment while instilling a sense of appreciation for nature. My school, as at many schools nationwide, began with environmental activities that center around Earth Day. The usual lessons on conservation, recycling and pollution were taught. My environmental education program grew from there and became more than just a once-a-year event with the creation of the Schoolyard Habitat environmental education program.

The Schoolyard Habitat environmental education program encompasses a planning process, hands-on activities, and real life experiences across the curriculum to develop a greater understanding of how we interact with natural resources. Awareness of environmental issues has evolved as students move toward environmental literacy. The Schoolyard Habitat environmental education program cultivates an understanding of how daily decisions, lifestyle choices, and recreational activities impact the Earth's finite resources.

Beginning an endeavor of the magnitude of a Schoolyard Habitat may seem overwhelming at first. Getting administration, [faculty,] staff, students, and parents onboard with the Schoolyard Habitat project is essential to the success. With the assistance of a friend and university professor, I began by putting together a proposal to present to the [faculty,] staff, and administration. Through research on environmental education I found a great deal of information on the importance of environmental literacy and the academic benefits of environmental education to the curriculum. Environmental education encompasses more than global warming and recycling. Today's students will face many environmental issues as they grow into productive members of society. Students will need to make well-informed decisions on these environmental issues. A Schoolyard Habitat provides opportunities for students to explore environmental issues across the curriculum. The state standards and the school's curriculum were matched with the outcomes of the Schoolyard Habitat program, providing a guide for the cross-curricular implementation of the habitat project. The schoolyard was measured and a map created of the habitat area. A plan of action for developing and maintaining the habitat area was made. A budget for funding the project, including school-provided funds, grants, and fundraisers, was calculated. The supporting research, curriculum components, plan of action, and budget were formatted into a booklet that was presented for approval to the administration and [faculty and] staff. Total commitment was needed for the project to succeed.

A Schoolyard Habitat gives a teacher the occasion to incorporate environmental learning into whatever subject area is being taught. Students monitored local media for the reporting on environmental matters. These matters were discussed as a part of current events or even circle time. The school library was stocked with trade books pertaining to environmental issues. Parents and members of the community who work for utility companies, waste management,

and land management were invited to come in to talk about their environmental programs. Our school sponsored environmentally friendly activities such as a recycling project, litter cleaning up, and water conservation in addition to starting a habitat restoration venture. Students designed the habitat, which made for a great math project. Students measured for the perimeter markings of the habitat. They calculated the area of the garden. The number of plants to order per square foot was determined. Next, the cost of materials was calculated. Finally, a plan for obtaining the necessary funds was developed. Getting the students involved in the planning process of the Schoolyard Habitat helped them to obtain a sense of ownership and pride in the project. It's really a chance for them to feel like they made a difference in the vast world ecosystem.

Many ecology activities accompany language arts, fine arts, and history, as well. Nature is a great topic for writing. Students observed the Schoolyard Habitat and then wrote poems, essays, and stories about what they observed. Parents built an outdoor classroom for students to work and make observations. Students studied the habitat and created works of art involving nature. Politics and government are good topics for bringing in environmental legislature. Students held debates over such legislature. As our school discusses heroes and world leaders, those who fought for environmental reform were included. Students made informational posters and signs and hung them near and around the habitat area to educate others on these important issues. Students were assigned topics and people related to environmental issues to research on the internet. Students then wrote research papers on their findings or created PowerPoint [presentations] to present their findings as a form of public speaking. Student work was published by displaying it throughout the school helping to educate the community on environmental issues. The River of Words is a nonprofit organization dedicated to connecting students to the environment through poetry and art. Our students submitted and won awards for works of art and poetry dealing with the subject of natural habitat.

Field trips were designed to get students involved with nature and to provide an opportunity for students to learn more about ecology. One of the teachers at our school set up a Garden Club. Members of the Garden Club work in the Schoolyard Habitat regularly to study and help the ecosystem, as well as to learn more about ecology from projects and guest speakers. Educators from environmental agencies, such as the [Maryland] Department of Natural Resources and the [Civilian] Conservation Corp, came into school to do projects with students to teach them about preserving the environment. The Schoolyard Habitat was a part of our various environmental endeavors that earned our school the Maryland Green School Award. The Maryland Green School Awards Program recognizes schools that prepare students to understand and act on current and future environmental challenges and implement projects and programs that result in a healthier environment.

The Schoolyard Habitat environmental education program has a great deal of benefits for any education system, be it a formal classroom setting or an informal experience. Environmental topics engage and create an enthusiasm for learning, which in turn fosters fewer discipline and classroom management problems, better testing scores, and real-world application of classroom learning.

Our Schoolyard Habitat project has been a great success. The project brought together the school and community for the betterment of the environment.

Wicomico Day School was recognized with an environmental education award. Teachers, staff, and students are acknowledged often for all they are doing to make the school green. Everyone's help is needed to make a difference in an endeavor such as this. As students are exposed to the wonders of nature more and more they will gain an appreciation for the environment. As students gain an appreciation for the environment they will want to learn about protecting ecosystems. As students desire to protect ecosystems they will be more likely to take actions to make a difference. My entire school is committed to ongoing environmental education in order to provide our students with a better understanding of today's environmental issues.

Stephanie Colby Lee[2]: Helping Students Become Green Kids

With as much as the curriculum has changed in my eight years of teaching sixth-grade science, I have always been fortunate enough to have an environmental science unit included within the scope of my curriculum. Instruction in environmental science is the perfect opportunity to immerse the students in their science content, but having the skill and finding the time to do so can often be difficult. In my fifth year at Westland Middle School, in an effort to become recognized as one of Maryland's Green Schools, we partnered up with the Audubon Naturalist Society in Chevy Chase and their Green Kids program. This yearlong relationship included naturalist support in the classroom with various explorations throughout the year.

When I first met with the Green Kids educator, she and I discussed the importance of establishing student interest and student buy-in for our efforts. We began our interactions with Audubon naturalists by completing the Life in a Square activity. [Authors' note: See Chapter 6 for a similar activity.] This activity was completed fairly early in the year and gave the students, who were all new to the school, their first opportunity to explore and evaluate the status of their new school environment. I was almost as excited as the students were to get outside and explore. After we had built up this energy and enthusiasm about exploring our school environment, the naturalist gave a presentation to the students, overviewing some of the various aspects of environmental science and presenting some possible action projects

---

[2]   Stephanie Colby Lee is a sixth-grade science teacher and team leader at Westland Middle School, Bethesda, MD; phone 301-320-6515.

Reflections on Implementation

that we could conduct within our school community. Following this presentation, the students completed a survey to help identify the projects that they were most interested in completing, and from those results we planned our instruction with the end goal of completing a grade-based multifaceted project.

It was a very interesting and validating experience for me as a teacher to be able to give my students the opportunity to reflect on an activity (Life in a Square) and use that experience to help determine the next steps they would be interested in taking. With the student survey indicating that the students were most interested in projects relating to runoff, we began by having students, in small groups, create their own watershed models in tin pans. It was messy, or at least wet, but by constructing and manipulating the model themselves I felt like they developed a deeper understanding and connection to the concept. We followed this individual modeling activity with explorations of runoff and an activity using an EnviroScape model (a tabletop model that provides an interactive learning experience—this one illustrates how the combined impact of pollution from a number of small sources can have a large effect on watershed health) to demonstrate

the concept and reinforce the importance of buffers. Though it was difficult to fit this activity fully into one class period, it was very encouraging to see how engaged the students seemed to be by the simple spraying of water on the EnviroScape as they witnessed the resulting runoff. It is one thing to discuss what runoff is and how it occurs; it is another to actually isolate the cause and effect in a microcosm like the EnviroScape. As the year progressed, we continued to have Green Kids educators deliver activities in our classes about once every six weeks. We completed additional activities, such as "Erosion in a Bottle" and "Who Polluted the Potomac?," which allowed the students to bring the concept of runoff to their level and to be able to manipulate it. Though both of these activities were messy and heavily loaded with materials preparation, the insight these learning experiences provided the students far outweighed the inconvenience of an untidy room.

Throughout the year as our Green Kids educators came in to present lessons, we slowly began to plan our culminating project. We knew that the students had an express interest in assessing the impact of runoff and developing methods to prevent it. As a result of this we settled on three different projects that the students would complete at the end of the year during our single-day, whole-grade, multiproject venture. Having multiple projects going at the same time posed a challenge and required a lot of additional support, but I was very fortunate to have the support of the Audubon Naturalist Society educators we'd worked with through the year, and even additional members from their staff. It was reaching out to these outside organizations that made the project more meaningful and manageable for me as a classroom teacher.

Since our sixth grade included about 230 students, we broke the students into two different groups based on their team assignment. One team worked on the projects in the morning, while the other team composed poems and illustrations for the River of Words competition. In the afternoon, the two teams switched. At one station the students made a direct connection to their studies as they planted trees as a buffer along the Little Falls Stream. As they completed the activity we reflected on connections between the various activities we had completed relating to buffers and the action we were taking. The second station gave the students an opportunity to evaluate the impact that runoff had made on their local stream, as they conducted water quality tests and macroinvertebrate sampling. At a third station the students were guided in the removal of non-native species, in an effort to provide more available habitat for native plants. The students were active and excited through each activity, and as their teacher it was very rewarding to see the enthusiasm my students displayed as they actively applied the knowledge we had built throughout the year.

While the project as a whole was a rewarding experience, both for students and science teachers, it was not without its difficulty or problems. Weather was always a concern, and it did present a real problem the second year we implemented the project. Choosing to complete the project at the end of the school year, we ran into a day with extreme heat that was not suitable for outdoor activity. This disruption to my well-organized plans was a source of great frustration, but not impossible to deal with. Another difficulty I experienced was in trying to gather support from some of my colleagues, other sixth grade teachers, as this would require a sacrifice of their instructional time. Keeping this in mind, we planned our culminating activity to take place after our exam week in hopes that it would be less disruptive to instruction. It was also quite helpful to have all of the additional outside support to be able to convince other sixth grade teachers that this project did not mean additional work for them.

In summary, I feel very strongly that the challenges that went along with planning our multi-project venture were well worth the effort. I highly recommend seeking support from environmental organizations, as it is a difficult undertaking for one person on his or her own. While I was fortunate to benefit from the support of the Audubon Naturalist Society, other organizations such as the [state] Department of Natural Resources or the Chesapeake Bay Foundation are also worth looking into for support with these valuable experiences.

R. Mark Herzog[3]: In the "Old Days" We Went Outside

As a student, a long time ago, I can remember (barely) wondering to myself why I enjoyed certain classes and why others seemed so painful to get through; why some teachers looked like they were having fun, while others seemed only to be going through the motions. One factor that seemed

obvious, even to me, even in elementary school, was that I liked it when teachers took me out of the building. Recess (I told you I was old) was obviously meant to be enjoyable and physical education classes, out on the fields, fit that bill as well, but there were a few occasions when there was an academic reason for getting out of those little one-piece desks and leaving the classroom, the hallway, and the building, and learning in a different place and a different way. I had only five field trip experiences in my 13 (I went to kindergarten) years of public school and they are all stored firmly in detail in my memory banks: the Carnegie Museum of Natural History in Pittsburgh (I can still see the teeth of that T-Rex skeleton); Brauns Bakery (I can still smell that fresh-baked bread); Fallingwater (Frank Lloyd Wright's cantilevered home in southwest Pennsylvania); the local township office building (my seventh-grade social studies teacher ran a mock election and I won the position of Solicitor, without really knowing what that was); and a 10-day trip to Germany (thanks to my brave tenth-grade German teacher). Because of those teachers and those experiences I now have increased interest in, and a better understanding of, archaeology, baked goods, architecture, politics, and travel.

---

[3]   R. Mark Herzog is the assistant supervisor of science for Harford County Public Schools and director of the Harford Glen Environmental Education Center, 502 West Wheel Road, Bel Air, MD 21015; phone 410-638-3903.

What were my other teachers doing during those same days and years? No idea. I'm sure they were nice people, doing a reasonable job at whatever they were hired to do, but I don't remember them. Can't picture them, their names or (with a few exceptions) any of their lesson plans. I have been a middle and high school science teacher for 20 years and a science supervisor for more than 10 and I have not found a better way to make an indelible impression on students than to take them somewhere, show them something interesting, and let them talk about it. It doesn't have to involve Lufthansa or even a bus ride (although I highly recommend both) to make that impression. Taking students, as I have done, to the school's courtyard and challenging them to bring back different species of plants growing in the "grass" compared with the football field leads nicely to an informed discussion/investigation into the relative benefits of diversity. Circumnavigating the school grounds and asking students, GPS units and field guides in hand, to map the landscape to scale, naming all of the species of plants (natives and non-natives); investigating where the rainwater goes and discovering subtle elevation variations that encourage flow in this direction and not that; proposing (always include the principal and custodians in such things),

designing, and creating ponds, gardens, or arboretum projects; or any of the other examples of fun and worthy activities listed in this book, can do for students what a few of my teachers did for me—produce a science-related memory that years from now will still make them smile and wonder, and maybe even become a science teacher or supervisor.

My current position in Harford County, Maryland, includes managing the school system's environmental education and residential center. My office is in a 200-year-old stone house, and the view out my windows includes two streams, lots of woods and, an active beaver dam. I love my job but, atmospherics aside, the greatest benefit, personally and professionally, is when I get to introduce elementary school students to nature and all that she offers. From the moment these nervous fifth graders step down from their bus and start looking around our facility they are immersed in the outdoors. They will sleep and eat and get oriented under roofs, but for the rest of the time they are with us (four days and three nights) they are outside being asked and asking questions about the environment. They ask a lot of questions! That's what real scientists do.

Getting out of the school building is a good teaching technique for a number of obvious reasons: the senses are put on a higher alert because of the novel surroundings; the boundaries for observation are typically expanded, therefore requiring more complex thinking; the lesson is automatically placed in a physical context with connections branching out in many directions; and perhaps most importantly, being outside underlines the reality of whatever is being studied. Inside a science classroom, the materials are prepared, the lab teams are appointed, the procedures are scripted and understood, the related textbook passages are read or referred to, but it all has an artificial feel to it. Students know that the teacher has to fit this "discovery lesson" into the prescribed number of minutes and they better have their aha moment and get the correct answer before the bell rings, or else. Outside, there may not be a right answer, or at least not one today. There may be unanticipated variables that the wind or the rain or the local wildlife brought into the process. Students need to be aware and wary when they step outside; they're not reading a textbook with predictable outcomes anymore. Nature's revelations frequently don't fit in a seven-period day or resolve into clear, clean, consistent answers to our questions. That's reality, and teaching students that lesson is important.

It is also gratifying and demonstrably effective. In our files, I have about 30 years worth of exit evaluation surveys from our residential program. Those surveys are filled in by parents, high school counselors who help run our fifth-grade program, the classroom teachers who come to stay overnight with their students, and the fifth graders themselves. The overwhelming percentage of responses is enthusiastically favorable for what we do. Terms like "eye-opening," "engaging," "great," and "wonderful" pepper the testimonials, and these same people come back to visit over the summer or in later years and want to tell me in person how much they appreciate the school system's efforts to go above and beyond for kids. And when those kids get to the end of their careers, in whatever profession they choose, I feel confident that stored in their memory banks will be vivid pictures of what they were doing and who they were with when they studied a small patch of nature in Maryland.

Why don't we do more of this? Largely because almost every aspect of it is currently inconvenient. Too little time, lack of funding, lack of equipment, too little teacher expertise or confidence, administrative skepticism, and lack of convenient, proximate spaces to explore. Many of the same reasons we don't stretch traditions and do a lot of potentially powerful instruction. All of these obstacles can be addressed or removed if a school system trusted in the benefits for children that accrue from just getting out.

Pamela Lottero-Perdue and Steven Lev[4]: A Science Educator and a Geologist Work Together to Make Topography Elementary

We conceptualized the activity "Constructing Essential Ideas of Topography" to engage children in using the tools of geologists and surveyors to map real-scale contour lines on a hill, giving children a direct and concrete experience to construct these essential ideas. What we describe here is how we—an elementary science specialist (Pam) and content specialist (Steve)—worked together to consider and modify the tools of the trade to make contour line mapping both accessible and accurate for elementary children.

During the lesson development stage of our activity, Steve brought two tools to Pam's office—the Jacob's staff and transit level. These are the tools that geologists and surveyors use to map the elevation of the Earth's surface. The transit level is a handheld device that is peered into with a single eye, showing an unmagnified view of its subject (i.e., the Jacob's staff) as well as a see-through bubble level. The Jacob's staff looks somewhat like a telescoping meter stick. Two individuals work together to determine elevation intervals, with the transit level used by one individual, and the bottom of the Jacob's staff held firmly against the ground by the other. A wide range of elevation intervals can be measured with these tools.

It became quickly apparent to us that while useful for experts in the field, these tools were likely to be expensive for teachers to purchase and awkward for children to use. A surveyor's transit level is relatively costly, can appear daunting to operate, and may present the same kinds of challenges as do microscopes, with teachers being uncertain as to whether or not children are seeing what it is that the teacher wants them to see. Furthermore, the Jacob's staff, with metric and English increments marked in tenths, was likely to present another challenge for children in consistently using the correct scale.

Although these professional tools were not elementary friendly, this

---

[4] Both Dr. Pamela Lottero-Perdue and Dr. Steven Lev are faculty members in the Department of Physics, Astronomy and Geosciences at Towson University, Towson, MD; phone 410-704-4598 for Dr. Lottero-Perdue and 410-704-2744 for Dr. Lev.

was not a barrier to lesson development. In the same way that elementary educators may use paper cups instead of beakers, build pinhole viewers out of shoeboxes, or conduct scratch tests with paper clips, we simply considered what other tools we might use. We did so with the help of a professional engineer who has experience with the kinds of levels used in home construction and manufacturing, Kevin Perdue (Pam's husband). These tools—a stake, a bullseye level, a string, and a line level—were accurate and simple to use and enabled children to construct contour lines and thus [convey] the essential ideas about topography we aimed to teach.

Teachers and elementary science specialists who wish to help children construct science concepts inside or outside the classroom would do well to consult with content experts, be they science professors at the university level, high school science teachers, engineers, or scientists in industry or the field. Their content knowledge coupled with the teacher's or science specialist's ability to make learning accessible to elementary children can make for a meaningful learning experience. The key to success, though, is mutual respect among professionals whose common goal it is to make science interesting and real to students. We achieved

this working relationship, and we hope that you do, too!

Debbie Freels[5]: "Where Are My Sneakers?"

Looking back at the last 29 years as an educator, my fondest memories are of the 4 years that I served as principal of William S. James Elementary School in Harford County, Maryland. I'm filled with pride as I remember how the teachers, students, and community bonded together to support the Governor's Green School initiative.

Growing up in Baltimore City, my concept of nature was limited to the bugs that crawled on and around the single tree in the front yard and the squirrels and robins that occasionally visited the same tree. Not having the experience of hiking in the woods, or looking for critters in a stream or pond, I grew up with a warped perception of our world, compared with the world as I know it today. Luckily, my experiences broadened while as a college student, I had the opportunity to venture on trips outside of the city. As a city girl, I was pleasantly surprised, shocked actually, that I enjoyed hiking on trails, seeing nature in bloom, hearing rippling

---

[5] Debbie Freels is a former principal and currently an elementary instructional facilitator at Magnolia Elementary School, Harford County, MD; phone 410-612-1553.

brooks and unseen animals, that I had not seen or heard before. It is these initial memories of me venturing out of my comfort zone that have fueled my desire to promote increasing environmental studies for students.

After teaching for 10 years and serving as an assistant principal for 7 years, I was promoted to principal of William S. James. The school was in the third year of implementation of Co-Nect, a comprehensive school reform model where students in multiage groups were taught the curriculum through authentic interdisciplinary projects. Many of the teachers were incorporating science into the projects, but one team of intermediate teachers had decided that all of their projects for the year would have an environmental theme. After conducting extensive research, this team of teachers and students designed and created a pond on the school grounds, complete with native plants, which later became an outdoor classroom for the entire school. As I watched this team of teachers work with third-, fourth-, and fifth-grade students, I was convinced that by teaching content area curriculum through the lens of science, that students were more engaged, more motivated to learn, and as a result performed at a higher level. This particular project demonstrated that students of all ability levels could be challenged to think critically, to problem solve and to work collaboratively with peers to create a positive change in the environment while learning and applying content knowledge.

During my second year of tenure as principal, William S. James became a Professional Development School (PDS) for Towson University; I was eager as the student interns in this cohort were all elementary education candidates with supplementary course work in math and science. With the additional support of the PDS, the School Improvement Plan was written to include a goal for all teachers in grades prekindergarten through fifth grade to incorporate science content into all projects. The interns, who were eager to experience the project-based teaching and even more eager to infuse additional science and mathematics content into the project, had a profound impact on the teaching staff. Teachers who had been more reluctant to venture outside of the classroom were now taking students outside of the building to teach. After observing a third-grade teacher and intern co-teach a lesson on measurement out on the field behind the school, I knew I had to keep a pair of sneakers in my office to be able to keep up with the faculty!

Reflections on Implementation

It became important to have regularly scheduled opportunities for teachers to share their projects and experiences with the entire faculty, as this fostered enthusiasm and creativity and opened the door for possibilities. Teachers began writing grants to acquire funding for field trips, classroom resources, and materials for the outdoor classroom. Working with Dr. Robert Blake, the coordinator for the PDS, teachers became acquainted with the Chesapeake Bay Foundation and were able to involve their students in bay restoration activities. All grade levels took field trips to Harford Glen, the school system's environmental and residential center, throughout the school year to support what they were learning in the classroom. Teams of teachers from several grade levels worked together to plan Earth Day initiatives, including a stream restoration and reforestation on the school grounds. This event was attended and celebrated by parents, community members, and school board and local officials. Our teachers and students were learning and demonstrating that their actions could have a positive impact on the entire community.

After four years of teaching students through science-oriented projects, state assessment results indicated that scores in both math and reading had risen from the bottom third to the top third of schools in the county. Not only were our teachers energized through this approach to teaching, but our students were demonstrating their ability to think critically, to problem solve, to be creative, to work collaboratively and to make a difference in the world. While all of us at William S. James were aware that our students were excelling, it was gratifying to know that the public was now aware of our success as well.

What Next?

The preceding narratives provide a glimpse into the success you can have with field-based learning and come from a breadth of stakeholders in the elementary and middle school settings. Although each writer comes from a different background (not necessarily as science majors or science teachers), each came to the same conclusion: Get kids outside learning. Our simple goal with this book is that you are encouraged to take your students outside the classroom to engage them in meaningful learning experiences in the field. While the science content presented may not be what you encountered in your high school or teacher preparation classes, with a little initiative we believe that you can know "more than enough" science and be comfortable as you engage your students in field-based science experiences. Our hope is that you too will add your story and tell how you and your students went outside, learned about the environment, and experienced the wonders that the world has to offer.

Resource List
Websites

Audubon Naturalist Society
*www.audubonnaturalist.org/RunScript.
asp?p=ASP\Pg0.asp*

Carnegie Museum of Natural History
www.carnegiemnh.org

Chesapeake Bay Foundation
www.cbf.org

EnviroScape (portable environmental
education models)
www.enviroscape.com

Maryland Department of Natural Resources
www.dnr.state.md.us

*www.dnr.maryland.gov/education/greenschools.
html* (Green School program)

Maryland State Department of Education
Professional Development School Network
http://cte.jhu.edu/PDS

National Wildlife Federation
www.nwf.org
*www.nwf.org/gardenforwildlife/certify.
cfm?campaignid=WH10PHPX* ("Certify Your
Wildlife Garden")

River of Words
www.riverofwords.org

Towson University Professional Development
School (PDS) Network
www.towson.edu/coe/pdsn

About the Authors

Robert W. Blake Jr. (Bob) grew up in Brockport, New York, ten miles from Lake Ontario and a few steps from the great outdoors. He spent his youth doing anything that kept him outside, including fishing, skiing, sailing, hunting, playing baseball, and taking long hikes in the surrounding fields and woods. He received his bachelor's degree in biology from SUNY Albany (1983) and, after three years of teaching skiing in Killington, Vermont, got master of arts in teaching degree in biology from Brown University (1988). In 1994 he attained a doctorate in curriculum design from the University of Illinois at Chicago. A former high school and middle school science teacher, Bob has been at Towson University since 1997, where he works with elementary preservice interns as they learn to teach science. He lives in Cockeysville, Maryland, with his wife, Jennifer, and his daughter, Mackenzie.

J. Adam Frederick grew up in Superior, Wisconsin, and Brockport, New York, and is a proud graduate of Slippery Rock University in Pennsylvania. Upon graduation he moved to Frederick, Maryland, and taught high school science courses while finishing his master's degree in environmental biology at Hood College. After teaching for nine years he began working with the Maryland Sea Grant Extension Program in Marine Education and has been a University of Maryland Extension faculty member for the past 15 years, working in the Center of Marine Biotechnology in Baltimore, Maryland. In 1990 he settled in Frederick with his wife, two sons, and daughter.

Sarah Haines grew up on the Eastern Shore of Maryland and first made her way to Pennsylvania to attend Bucknell University in Lewisburg, Pennsylvania. After attending graduate school at the University of Georgia and earning master's and doctoral degrees in zoology, she returned to Maryland to teach middle school and earn a master's degree in education from Salisbury University. In 2000, she settled in the Baltimore area with her husband and two young sons. She joined the faculty of Towson University in August 2000 as an assistant professor and is now an associate professor and the director of the Center for Science & Mathematics Education at Towson University.

Stephanie Colby Lee grew up in Silver Spring, Maryland, and attended Montgomery County Public Schools. After completing her undergraduate studies in elementary education, with a concentration in mathematics and science, at Towson University, she returned to the school system that educated her and began teaching sixth-grade science at Westland Middle School in Bethesda, Maryland, where she currently serves as one of the sixth-grade team leaders. During her nine years at Westland, Stephanie has been a sponsor of the BaySavers club, mentor to teacher interns, and recipient of the Marian Greenblatt Excellence in Teaching Award as one of three teachers nominated for Montgomery County Teacher of the Year in 2007. Stephanie resides in Silver Spring with her husband, John, and enjoys spending time with family, reading, kayaking, and playing soccer.

Figure Credits

The following photos are courtesy of J. Adam Frederick: bloodroot (p. xi), yearbook photo of Mary E. E. Kready (p. xii), Towson University preservice teachers (p. xiv); teachers (p. xvii), Western River Valley (p. 2), Google Earth screen-cap (p. 5), Towson University preservice intern (p. 15), aerial photo (p. 45), rain forest, desert, and mountain (p. 46), macroinvertebrate (p. 47), mountain spring (p. 49), jellyfish (p. 50), soil (p. 69), soil percolation (p. 80), sunset (p. 85), and spider (p. 109).

The following figures are courtesy of J. Adam Frederick: Figures 1.1, 1.2, 1.3, 1.5, 1.9, 1.10, 1.11, 1.14, 2.1, 2.2, 2.3, 2.4, 2.5, 2.6 (redrawn with permission from Maryland Department of Natural Resources), 2.7, 2.9, 2.11, 2.12, 2.13, 3.1, 3.3, 3.5, 3.6 (redrawn with permission), 3.7 (redrawn with permission), 3.8 (redrawn with permission), 3.9, 3.10, 3.12, 3.13, 3.14, 3.15, 3.16, 3.17, 3.18, 3.19, 3.20, 3.21, 3.22, 3.23, 3.24, 4.2, 4.3, 4.5, 4.6, 4.8, 4.9, 4.10, 4.11, 4.12, 4.13, 4.14, 4.15, 5.2, 5.3, 5.4, 5.5, 5.6, 5.7, 5.8, 5.10, 5.11, 5.12, 5.13, 5.15, 5.16, 5.17, 5.18, 6.1, 6.2, 6.3, 6.4, 6.5, 6.6, 6.7, 6.8, 6.9, 6.11, 6.12, 6.13, 6.14, 6.15, and 6.16.

The following are courtesy of Robert W. Blake, Jr.: elementary students in field (pp. xix, 125) and Figures 7.3, 7.5, 7.7, and 7.8.

The following are courtesy of Sarah Haines: Figures 7.1, 7.2, 7.4, and 7.6.

The following are courtesy of Pamela Lottero-Perdue: Figures 1.6, 1.7, 1.8, 1.15, 1.16, 1.17, 1.18, 1.19, 1.20, 1.21, and 1.22.

Index

*Page numbers in **boldface** type refer to figures or tables.*

Index

Index

Index

Index